THE MEMOIRS OF
WILLIAM JENNINGS BRYAN

KENNIKAT PRESS SCHOLARLY REPRINTS

Dr. Ralph Adams Brown, Senior Editor

Series in
AMERICAN HISTORY AND CULTURE
IN THE NINETEENTH CENTURY
Under the General Editorial Supervision of
Dr. Martin L. Fausold
Professor of History, State University of New York

WILLIAM JENNINGS BRYAN
From the painting by Irving R. Wiles in the State Department at Washington.

THE MEMOIRS OF
WILLIAM JENNINGS BRYAN

BY HIMSELF AND HIS WIFE
MARY BAIRD BRYAN

Volume I

KENNIKAT PRESS
Port Washington, N. Y./London

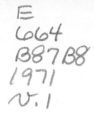

THE MEMOIRS OF WILLIAM JENNINGS BRYAN

First published in 1925
Reissued in 1971 by Kennikat Press
Library of Congress Catalog Card No: 73-137904
ISBN 0-8046-1472-5

Manufactured by Taylor Publishing Company   Dallas, Texas

KENNIKAT SERIES ON AMERICAN HISTORY AND
CULTURE IN THE NINETEENTH CENTURY

INTRODUCTION

By Mary Baird Bryan

IT has fallen to me to take up the pen which Mr. Bryan laid down.

In justice to him, it should be borne in mind that his chapters are in the first draft; he had no opportunity to revise or polish them.

While I am willing to carry out his ideas, the fact remains that it is impossible for me, or for anyone else, to do this work as he had planned it. The intimate knowledge of people and of small happenings has passed with him.

However, from his private correspondence, from his documents, and from my diary, I hope to bring to light the truth on several controversial questions.

I wish, too, to give a careful and just analysis of his character. His dominant traits will explain his course of action in several crises.

In this work I have been assisted in research and collation by our children, by other members of the family, by faithful friends, and by the competent staff which was furnished me by the Publishers.

Mary B. Bryan

CONTENTS

CONTENTS

PART I

PREFACE

By William J. Bryan

IN giving the public the story of my life I trust I may be credited with something more than a desire to acquaint the public with myself. The time has passed when I could have any ulterior motive in a heart-to-heart talk with the American people. Whatever ambition I have had has been more than gratified; I feel that I have received more than I have deserved and been abundantly repaid for the efforts I have made in behalf of the American people.

It is my purpose to show that in my own case good fortune has had more to do with such success as I may have achieved than any efforts of my own. Success in politics—and, to a large extent in other lines of activity—is the conjunction of opportunity and the preparedness to meet it. Opportunity comes independently of one's own efforts; and his preparedness to meet opportunity is due, as I shall show, largely to others. The facts as I present them will prove that I have been wonderfully fortunate in the opportunities that have come to me and that I am indebted to a multitude of individuals known and unknown for such preparation as I have had to improve the opportunities as they came.

My second purpose is to show the goodness of the American people, their patriotism, their moral courage, their high ideals, their willingness to sacrifice for their convictions—the virtues that not only make popular government possible but insure its success. No man in public life has ever been in a better position to record these virtues of the people or under deeper obligation to give them the credit they deserve.

I trust that with the two purposes in view I may be able so to shift the accent from "I" to "they" as to purge my Memoirs of every trace of egotism or self-assertion. I shall

9

relate my own connection with individuals, measures, and events, but I shall endeavor so to interweave the actions of others with my own acts as to make the results appear as the result of a joint effort in which I have played but a part, and often but an inconsequential part.

In politics as in the army, the generals receive the glory while the enlisted men die in the trenches. The names that are prominent become household words, while the multitude who bear the burden are nameless in history.

That which was called Bryanism in derision by many, represented a group of substantial reforms; it was not an individual thing but rather the result of united effort of some six and a half millions of American voters. I was but one of the millions, but because I was in a position of leadership I received the glory and the censure, while others equally earnest and often with more sacrifice labored and died unknown to fame.

To begin the story of my good fortune. I was born in the greatest of all ages. No golden ages of the past offered any such opportunity for large service and, therefore, for the enjoyment that comes from consciousness that one has been helpful.

I was born a member of the greatest of all the races— the Caucasian Race, and had mingled in my veins the blood of English, Irish, and Scotch. One has only to consider the limitations upon one's opportunities imposed by race to understand the incalculable benefit of having the way opened between the child and the stars.

I was born a citizen of the greatest of all lands. So far as my power to prevent was concerned, I might have been born in the darkest of the continents and among the most backward of earth's peoples. It was a gift of priceless value to see the light in beloved America, and to live under the greatest of the republics of history.

And I was equally fortunate, as I shall show, in my family environment. I cannot trace my ancestry beyond the fourth generation and there is not among them, so far as I know, one of great wealth or great political or social prominence, but so far as I have been able to learn, they were honest, industrious, Christian, moral, religious people —not a black sheep in the flock, not a drunkard, not one for whose life I would have to utter an apology. The environment in which my youth was spent was as ideal as any that I know.

At the age of fourteen I became a member of the Church, as the result of a spiritual awakening that took place in the little town in which I was born. I shall elaborate upon it in the proper place in my story; I mention it now because it has had more influence in my life for good than any other experience, and I have been increasingly grateful for the circumstances that led me to take a stand on religion before I left home for college. It was of incalculable value to me during the period of questioning that seems unavoidable in the life of students. The influences of the Church, the Sunday school, the prayer meeting and the Y. M. C. A. were about me and sustained me until my feet were upon the Solid Rock and my faith built upon an enduring foundation.

I have often been reminded of one of the concluding verses of the Twenty-third Psalm: "Thou preparest a table before me in the presence of mine enemies." And still more frequently do I recall that wonderfully expressive description of superlative blessings: "My cup runneth over." If judging the future by the past can be made the basis of a firm hope, I can say, "Surely goodness and mercy shall follow me all the days of my life."

No one has been the recipient of as large a measure of unselfish devotion; no one is in better position to record with grateful appreciation the kindnesses received. I have never been in a position to repay friends in a political way. During my first term in Congress, the Republicans were in control of the national administration, so that I had no patronage at my command. During my second term in Congress, I was not in harmony with President Cleveland on the money question and soon ceased to be influential in the securing of appointments. Thus, during the four years in office in the earlier part of my life, I was unable to pay my debts with lucrative positions or to secure support by the hope of appointments. Even when I was Secretary of State, as I shall later relate, I was not able to reward any considerable number of political friends. My debts were larger and, in an appointive way, my assets smaller than those of any other cabinet member. All of the clerical force of the State Department is under the Civil Service, as are also the Consular offices. There are but a handful of assistants in the whole office who hold appointing power. Our ambassadors and ministers are largely chosen upon recommendation of the United States Senators.

And yet, while during the six years and three months of my official life I was practically powerless to reward those who had contributed to my success, I am sure that no one in this country—probably no one who ever lived—has had more friends, kept them for a longer period or received from them greater loyalty or more constant support. I have reason to know that the masses are patriotic and incorruptible. They cannot be purchased and they cannot be terrified. No matter how they may err or be led astray, the American people are sound at heart. They have solved successfully all problems that confronted them during the momentous years of our nation's history and there is not the slightest reason to doubt that they will meet every emergency, rise to every responsibility and prove that their capacity for self-government is as undeniable as their right to self-government.

The story of my life is but an account of opportunities improved and of circumstances of which I have taken advantage, but for the wisdom to see opportunities and the ability to take advantage of circumstances, I am indebted

12

PREFACE

to others more largely than to myself. In tracing my life from the beginning up to the time of the completion of this volume, I am simply showing what anyone, equally fortunate and with equal opportunities, can accomplish in this favored land of ours in this golden age.

If to the encouragement that my words may bring to the young men of our land I can add a moral, it is this: Truth, being of God, is omnipotent. It has within itself the power to propagate itself. Man may delay, but cannot prevent its triumph. Man borrows more strength from a great truth than he gives to it. It is of little importance to truth whether any individual espouses it, but to the individual it is of vital importance that he shall know the truth and, knowing it, adhere to it.

Jefferson said that he had learned that firm adherence to principle was the best handmaiden, even unto ambition.

If my Memoirs prove of benefit to others they will pay in part the debt I owe to those who in the past have contributed to the spread of the Christian religion, the safeguarding of society, and the establishing of popular government—the causes to which the mature years of my life have been dedicated.

CHAPTER I

IN THE BEGINNING

I WAS born on the nineteenth day of March, 1860, at Salem, Illinois. A picture of my birthplace to be found among the illustrations shows the house in which I first saw the light. The house stood on Broadway about halfway between the public square and the Baltimore and Ohio Railroad—prior to 1872 called the Ohio and Mississippi. It had never been materially changed from the time when it was built in 1852. My father, then a young lawyer just starting in at the practice, helped to hew the timbers to build the house. Being thus doubly attached to the homestead, I purchased it and gave it to the city of Salem, moving it a few feet to the west in order to give room for the erection of the Bryan Bennett Library, to which reference will be made in another chapter.

I do not know the hour of my birth, because the hour never became material until after the death of my parents. As soon as I was nominated for the Presidency, astrologists made their appearance and offered to consult my horoscope with a view to ascertaining whether I would be elected. I never had any faith in their calculations but, complying with my general rule, gave the specialists along various lines such information as I could furnish. I remember that one astrologer wrote a letter which my wife answered in my absence. He asked for the hour of the birth both of Mrs. Bryan and myself. She responded giving the day of my birth and the day and hour of her birth. Her parents were then residing with us and she was able to secure the information desired. The astrologer cast my horoscope, based upon such facts as he had, and declared that it indicated my election. He was very much mortified at my defeat—seemingly more than I was myself—and hastened to explain to Mrs. Bryan that his failure was due wholly to the fact that she did not give the exact hour of my birth. Having the hour of her birth, he had, since the election, cast her horoscope and felt sure that I would be yet elected for the Presidency. My wife enjoyed the humor of it and informed me that if I would stick to her she would land me in the White House yet. I responded, expressing my appreciation but admitting it was a little mortifying for a Presidential candidate to keep his horoscope in his wife's name.

I did not, until after the Chicago convention, hear much about the incidents of my childhood. I only know that I was blessed with as happy an environment as a child could hope for or ask. The two older children, John and Virginia, had died before the third child was born. As she was a daughter, I became the oldest son and had all the care that a mother could bestow upon a child and all the interest that a father could feel. A letter written just after my birth conveyed to the distant relative at whose home I lived while in college the fact of my birth. My father, who was suffering from a serious attack of diabetes, wrote to this relative that the birth of a son had increased his desire to live.

After my nomination, I met a Salem friend who told me that he had visited our home when I was just beginning to walk. It was evening and they were getting me ready for bed. According to this friend, my father stood me up before the visitor, and boastingly remarked, "He will be President some day." As my father never divulged to me any such expectations, I will be pardoned for considering the remark apocryphal.

The first thing that I can recollect is the younger child, Harry, crawling upon the floor. As he died when less than a year old, I could not have been more than three. My next recollection is of looking at the corpse of a neighbor who was a minister. They lifted me up so that I could see his face.

IN THE BEGINNING

According to family tradition, I was not a perfect child by any means, unless the word "perfect" is used to describe a boy with all the natural inclinations to mischief. Tradition has it that I used to disobey the injunctions of my mother and slip away from home to play with other children. Our yard was enclosed with the old-fashioned paling fence with a baseboard about a foot deep. By crawling close to the ground, I could conceal myself behind this broad board and thus get to the side of the fence without being noticed. More than once I was brought back and chastised and tied to the bed-post as a punishment.

MY AMBITIONS BEFORE SIX

Three ambitions entered into my life before I was six years old—I fix the age at six because one of the first things to stay in my memory is the removal to our farm home which occurred in the summer of 1866. The incidents of my boyhood are roughly classified as having occurred while we lived in town or after we moved to the country. That is the way I know of these three early ambitions. The first was to be a Baptist preacher—due doubtless to the fact that my father was a member of that church. Of course, I was too young to have any distinct recollection of either this ambition or its abandonment, but the record as given by my parents is that my father took me to an immersion one night during a protracted meeting held in a Christian Church. I saw the convert going down into the pool of water to be baptized. I evidently watched the ceremony with great interest and was deeply impressed by it. On my return home, I asked my father whether it would be necessary for me to go down into the pool of water in order to be a Baptist preacher. He answered in the affirmative, and after that they never could get me to say that I was "going to be a Baptist preacher." I do not know that any conclusion can be drawn from this incident unless it be that at this early age my parents had impressed upon me the virtue of truthfulness and that therefore I was not willing to avow an ambition from which I had been turned by fear of water.

My second ambition was to be a farmer and raise pumpkins. This did not last long, but long enough to be a matter of remark in the family. It may have been due to the plans we were making to remove to the country. I remember that a young lady by the name of Hester, daughter of Brother Williams, the much beloved pastor of the Christian Church, came into my life about that time and promised to wait for me. She was a very handsome girl, nearly grown, and encouraged me in my taste for agricultural pursuits. When I shortly afterwards decided to be a lawyer, she gave my change of plans as an excuse for refusing to look forward to a life partnership, and married a farmer cousin of mine.

My third ambition was probably due to the fact that my father was a lawyer, and at that time a circuit judge. I used to go down to the courthouse and sit upon the steps leading up to the bench and listen to the trial of cases. This ambition was more permanent than the ones which it succeeded. It remained with me during my school days and my college days, as the reader will see if he follows this narrative.

MY ANCESTRY

Ancestry counts. We inherit more than we ourselves can add. It means much to be borne of a race with centuries of civilization back of it. Blood, if it be good, inspires one to great effort—if it be bad it may paralyze ambition and fix the boundary to one's possibilities. I am speaking of the rule, not of the rare exceptions; many have become degenerate in spite of inheriting the stimulus to better things, and a few have, to a degree, overcome handicaps of their life and early environment.

If one is tempted to boast that he is self-made, a few reflections will puncture his pride. Let him analyze him-

18

self, separate all that has come to him into three factors: one representing that which has come to him by inheritance; another representing that which has entered his life through environment; and the third representing what he can fairly credit to himself—that which is not based upon either inheritance or environment—and the third factor will not be large enough to flatter his vanity.

The child comes into the world without its own volition, containing within himself capacities and weaknesses for which he is in no way responsible; he finds himself in an environment which he did not choose and cannot control. His first impressions come to him with breath and his life is largely moulded for him before he has intelligence to choose or standards by which to measure effort.

It is a consciousness of the helplessness of the new-born babe and of his dependence upon an unknown past and upon surroundings that he cannot comprehend that makes me increasingly grateful for the parentage with which the Heavenly Father blessed me and for the home in which my life began.

My father, Silas Lillard Bryan, was of Irish extraction. I do not know from what part of Ireland his ancestors came, nor when they crossed the ocean. I learned this since his death from a biographical sketch which I have reason to believe was written by him or submitted to him for his approval. William Bryan is the most remote forefather of whom I have knowledge. He lived in what was then a part of Culpeper (now Rappahannock) County and near the town of Sperryville, Virginia. He owned a tract of timber land in the Blue Ridge Mountains of which we learned when I was a young man because of a ninety-nine-year lease which expired about that time. We knew nothing of William Bryan's parents, brothers, or sisters. He belonged to the Baptist Church in that neighborhood, which was known as the Bryan Meeting House.

I digress at this point long enough to relate the experience

19

which I have had with my name. I had scarcely entered upon the practice of law when my business brought me into acquaintance with a number of people of Irish birth who frequently addressed me as "Mr. O'Brien." I was at first in doubt as to whether I should correct the mistake or allow it to pass unnoticed, but, deciding that honesty was the best policy, I said to a very typical son of the Emerald Isle, "My name is not O'Brien, but Bryan."

"It's all the same," he replied. "When Bryan Boru became king his descendants put on the 'O.' The Bryans are the same stock, but just common people."

I have had frequent occasion to use this explanation. The most notable opportunity was a dinner in Ireland tendered me by the Mayor of Dublin in 1903. One of the speakers jestingly called upon me to tell when I had dropped the "O." I replied by asking whether any of them ever knew of an O'Brien prior to the line of King Bryan Boru. When no one could name an earlier O'Brien, I explained to them that Bryan was the original name and that the "O" had been *added* by them, not eliminated by my ancestors.

After the campaign of 1896 I received a letter from a man in California named Bryan. He sent me an interview which he had given to the newspapers.

It seems that some one had claimed to have seen my name printed as "O'Brien" when I began the practice of law at Jacksonville, Illinois. My correspondent had given out an interview denying that there had been any change in my name and saying that he was a relative of mine. He explained to me that he was not a relative, but added that it was a poor friend that could not lie for another.

We know nothing of the parents, brothers, or sisters of William Bryan, my great-grandfather, and therefore have been unable to answer a multitude of questions which have been asked from time to time, the most persistent being whether our ancestor was related to the wife of Daniel

IN THE BEGINNING

Boone, whose maiden name was Bryan. William Bryan had three sons, Aquilla, James, and John. Aquilla Bryan, the oldest of the three sons, left Sperryville before or soon after my father's birth, to try his fortune in the Great West which was then inviting adventurers. When he reached the Ohio River the water was so high that instead of descending the river as he had intended, he crossed into Ohio and then waited for the waters to subside. That is the last knowledge we have of him that is authentic. We have met persons who with varying degrees of uncertainty thought they traced their ancestry back to this Aquilla Bryan, but no connection has been established with certainty.

James, the second son, went to Kentucky and located at Glasgow, where some of the family still reside.

John Bryan, my father's father, moved from his birthplace to Point Pleasant in what is now West Virginia. There my father spent part of his boyhood, but his mother died when he was twelve and his father when he was fourteen years old and Silas was entrusted to the care of different members of the family. His oldest brother, William Bryan, to whom I am indebted for the first part of my name, located on a farm near Troy, Missouri, where some of his descendants still live. Russell Bryan, his younger brother, located at Salem, where he raised a numerous family. His children were among my earliest playmates and most beloved companions.

John Bryan, my grandfather, was married to Nancy Lillard, a member of an English family. They lived in Culpeper County. This family was quite large and made up of men and women of character and virtue. My father was named after Silas Lillard, his mother's brother. When I went to Washington as a Member of Congress, I visited Virginia and became acquainted with a number of members of the Lillard family between whom and myself there grew up and has continued a warm friendship.

21

WILLIAM JENNINGS BRYAN

MY FATHER

As none of the brothers or sisters of my father were rich, he had the advantage of having to work. I do not know that this spur of necessity was absolutely necessary, but it is no disadvantage and it is possibly the best insurance against the influences that sap the energies and industry of young men. He had caught from some one the ambition to learn and though he had to work his way through school, he went further than any of his brothers or sisters in the pursuit of learning. When he was far enough advanced to teach he earned, by teaching, the money necessary to complete his college course, which was taken at McKendree College, Lebanon, Illinois. He had intended to attend a Baptist college, but for some reason changed his plans and entered the Methodist college above named. He took the classical course, graduating in 1849, and was always an enthusiastic believer in classical education for the young. He was a good student and interested also in the literary societies.

As father did not graduate until he was twenty-seven, he was one of the older students, although the age of graduation was probably older then than now. I have had the good fortune to meet several persons who were schoolmates of my father at Lebanon. From these I have learned something of my father as a student.

One incident seems to have made an impression at the time. Father used tobacco—I do not know in just what form at this time, later in life before he quit it entirely he indulged in chewing, smoking, and the use of snuff. He was in the habit of chewing tobacco while he was a student, as I learned from the following incident. Some teacher from another college made a speech to the boys. In the course of the address, the speaker commented upon the use of tobacco, criticizing it quite strongly, paying special attention to chewing. My father thought from what the speaker said he was making personal reference to him—whether true or not I do not know—but at the conclusion of the address father arose and made a speech in defense of the use of the weed. Later in life he became convinced that the use of tobacco was harmful, and just before the date of my birth he quit its use in every form. We thought it responsible for the dyspepsia which manifested itself about 1859 and continued to afflict him sorely until his death twenty-one years later.

Father was a very devout Christian. Just when he joined the Church I do not know, but it was probably at an early age. There came a day, however, when he was a young man, when religion took a very strong hold upon him and held him and became a controlling influence in his life. As a young man he was fond of fun and took delight in the frivolities of his day. One night as he went to a party he took cold and the cold developed into pneumonia. His condition finally became so critical that the attending physician thought it wise to inform him that, while his life was not despaired of, it would be the part of wisdom for him to make such provision for the future as he might think best. When the physician retired, father prayed as he had never prayed before and promised the Heavenly Father that if restored to health he would pray three times a day as long as he lived. He was restored to health and kept the promise.

I knew there was some such incident in his life, but did not learn the details until many years after his death and a few years after my mother's death. The facts were related to me by a caller who lived at one of the county seats which father visited when he was on the Circuit bench. My informant was then a boy and noticing that Judge Bryan bowed his head upon the desk when the noon whistle blew, asked his father why he did so. His father replied, "Judge Bryan is going to eat with us today and you had better ask him for an explanation." When the guest was at the table and the boy hesitated about asking the question, the father came to the boy's rescue and explained to Judge Bryan what the boy had noticed and asked the question the boy had intended to ask. Father moved his chair back from the table and said, "I am glad to answer the question," and then related the incident as it was told to me by the man, then the boy in the story.

This thrice-a-day prayer is the basis upon which numerous elaborations have been built. After my nomination for the Presidency a great many stories were told, differing in detail but all emphasizing the devotional side of my father's life. One story was that he opened court with prayer. Another, that he always prayed for guidance before rendering a decision. The first was not true, but knowing as I do his dependence upon God for guidance, I have no doubt that he invoked aid when entering upon anything important. I may add that my father's attitude on spiritual matters made a very deep impression upon me. There was a family altar in our house and the children were brought up according to the strictest views in religious matters, and my gratitude for such a home environment increased with the years. I shall be happy if my children feel toward me in mature life as I feel toward my father; if they revere my name as I revere my father's name and feel as deeply indebted to me for whatever there is in me of good.

After graduation at the age of twenty-seven, my father moved to Salem, the county seat of Marion County, Illinois, in which two of his sisters lived. At the age of twenty-nine he was admitted to the bar and about the same time or possibly a little earlier was elected superintendent of schools of that county. He began the practice of law in 1851 and in 1852 was elected to the Senate of the State of Illinois, where be served for eight years. He soon became prominent at the bar and prominent also as a public speaker. In 1860, at the age of thirty-eight, he was elected a judge of the Circuit that included about half a dozen counties and was re-elected in 1866, serving until 1872.

IN THE BEGINNING

In 1869 he was elected a member of the Constitutional Convention of Illinois and assisted in the drafting of that constitution. After his death I found in his library two volumes containing a record of the proceedings of the Constitutional Convention. On the fly leaf of the first volume I found a dedication of the books to myself. I immediately examined it, desiring to see what part he took, and was interested to find that at the very beginning of the session he introduced a resolution which reads as follows:

"*Resolved*, By the Convention: First—That all officers to be provided for in the new Constitution in the executive, legislative, and judicial departments, shall be elected by the people. Second—That the compensation to be allowed for official service in the several departments of the government shall be fixed in the Constitution, and shall not be increased or lessened by the legislative department."

It interested me to know that he shared Jefferson's confidence in the capacity of the people for self-government as well as in their right to self-government. He believed in entrusting them with their own affairs, as this resolution indicated. I have credited him with a definite influence in the shaping of my religious views; I am also indebted to him for the trend of my views on some fundamental questions of government, and have seen no reason to depart from the line he marked out.

My father was married at the age of thirty to Mariah Elizabeth Jennings, who had been one of his pupils when he taught school at Walnut Hill, Illinois. Mother was twelve years younger than father and had been his pupil when as a college student he was teaching in the Walnut Hill District, Walnut Hill being in the southeast corner of Marion County, twelve miles from Salem and about four from Centralia. Mother did not have the educational advantages father had secured, but she was as enthusiastic as he in her appreciation of education and in her devotion to it. Her studies after marriage and her companionship with him enabled her to make up somewhat for the shortness of her school days.

My Mother

But before speaking further of my mother, let me add a word here in regard to her lineage. As her maiden name indicated, she was of English ancestry, although, like my father's people, her family had been in the country so long, they were not able to trace any of them to the water's edge. The first of the Jennings of whom we have definite knowledge was Israel, my mother's grandfather. He moved to Illinois from Maysville, Kentucky, early in the eighteenth century and lived to a ripe old age, I think about a hundred years. Family tradition has it that he went from Maryland to Kentucky. His wife, Mary Waters, was a native of Maryland, but we have not been able to locate definitely any of her antecedents and but few of her collateral relatives. Israel Jennings had a large family, most of whom grew up in the neighborhood of Walnut Hill and Centralia.

My mother's mother was a Davidson and this family, too, had been in the United States long enough to lose its old-world connections. The Davidsons were of Scotch descent. Some of the family had been looking up the record recently and they found that there was a certain plaid that was worn by the Davidsons who, though not constituting a clan, were members of a clan. The earliest Davidson of whom we have a record lived in Virginia and went from there to Kentucky. From Kentucky the Davidsons, like the Jennings, moved to southern Illinois, evidently about the same time. I do not know whether it was because of the superiority in the attractiveness of the members of the two families or because of the scarcity of the population, but it is a rather remarkable fact that four Jennings married four Davidsons.

Mother was born on May the 24th, 1834, at Walnut Hill, a rural community near Centralia, Marion County, Illinois. She was reared in the country and attended the public school in the neighborhood. She was married at the age of eighteen (1852) and began housekeeping in the home on Broadway, about halfway between the public square and the railroad. Father helped to hew out the timbers and build their house. The style of it was that which was customary in that day. It had a room on each side of a short central hall, with two rooms upstairs over these lower rooms and a dining room and kitchen in the rear. In this house, the first six children were born. The two older children, Virginia and John, died of whooping cough before the third child was born. Frances, the next child, was born on March 18, 1858. My birthday came on the 19th of March, 1860, two years and one day later. The fifth child, Hiram, called Harry, died in infancy, and the sixth one, Russell, died at the age of seventeen. In 1866, the summer after I reached the age of six, we moved to the farm, about a mile northwest of the center of Salem, where the three younger children, Charles Wayland, Nancy Lillard, and Mary Elizabeth, were born.

Mother was a very competent woman, of rare native ability, of lofty ideals, and as devout as my father. While during the first twenty years of their married life they were members of different churches, there was never the slightest religious discord in the family and I never heard a word said in regard to the differences between denominations. Both of them were firmly wedded to the fundamentals of Christianity, but charitable on all nonessentials. This liberality in the matter of denominations was early impressed upon my mind by the family gatherings. It was in the old days of simple social customs when family dinners emphasized companionship and friendly intercourse rather than elaborate bill of fare. We were in the habit of having all the ministers at our home once a year and I knew all the ministers as "Brother."

While religious subjects occupied a prominent place in the conversation, the meals were not without a sprinkling of humor. I remember on one occasion that the meat for the dinner consisted of a roasted kid. As the plates were being served the conversation turned on the various kinds of meat and the Methodist preacher, Brother Mosser, expressed himself quite strongly as liking all kinds of meat excepting goat meat. Father had spoken of the meat as a roast, without designating the kind of animal that furnished it. After Mr. Mosser's statement he purposely avoided the subject until Brother Mosser was well through with a second helping, when the company enjoyed the joke.

My attitude on the subject of religious tolerance has been inherited, so to speak, from my parents. In memory of these religious social gatherings my good wife has been led to set aside certain days for the bringing together of the representatives of the various denominations in a social way.

I also received from my parents the impressions that have controlled my views on the husband's relation to the mother-in-law. When my father built the commodious brick house in which he lived upon the farm, one room was known as Grandma's room. At that time, my mother's mother was in good health with the prospect of living to a ripe old age. But although my mother's family was one of the largest among the children, it was always understood that Grandma was to have a home in our family if she reached an age when it was not desirable for her to continue to occupy the old homestead at Walnut Hill. The children expected some day to have my mother's mother as a member of the family, and the time came when she was too old to keep house any longer and came to spend her declining years with us. She lived to be more than eighty and it was a pleasure to minister to her during her years of feebleness.

When my wife's parents came to live with us, I recalled this early experience and the respect shown by my father to the mother of his wife. My wife's mother lived with us from 1884 to the spring of 1896 and my wife's father till 1905, and they were welcome members of our family.

My mother had not carried the study of music to the point where she practiced regularly, but she was proficient enough to play many instrumental selections and to play the accompaniment when she sang. Some of the tunes still run through my mind and the words of the songs are still recalled. "When you and I were young, Maggie," was popular at that time, and the war song, "Farewell, Mother, you may never press me to your heart again." The words came back to me when I was for a little while a soldier and I found myself time and again humming the tune that I had heard her sing when I was a boy.

My father being absent at court a considerable portion of the time, the burden of directing the family affairs and taking full control of the children fell upon her. Every duty was faithfully discharged. As I look back upon those early days, I cannot recall a single word that she ever said or a single act of hers that to me seems worthy of criticism. I feel that she was as nearly a perfect wife and mother as one could be. When father died, her oldest child was twenty-two, I was twenty, and the youngest child was ten. She assumed with courage the double responsibility of being to the children both mother and father. She survived my father sixteen years and lived to see her children grown, settled, and successful in life, and was revered by all of them. As a mother, she had one advantage that can hardly be overestimated. Her husband set an example in word and conduct that she could always invoke in the training of the children. Not in a single matter was it necessary to warn the children against following their father's example. Thus the memory of the two is entwined as if of a single character, so much alike were they in all that contributed to character building.

In 1872 my mother took her letter from the Methodist Church to the Baptist Church and from that time until her death became more and more a defender of the creed of that church, though she never carried it to the point of criticizing the doctrines of any other denomination. She had a sense of humor that relieved the conversation in the home. As my father also turned occasionally to the lighter vein and indulged in stories that had a point, I am not sure to which one I am most indebted for my fondness of the stories which I have used in abundance in my speeches. As I proceed with the narrative of my own life, I shall have occasion to refer from time to time to things that my parents said. At this time, I venture to illustrate their sense of humor by two stories for which I am indebted to them.

Some years ago I met an old resident of Salem who had often heard my father speak. Having heard me use in a lecture a story in connection with prohibition, he said it reminded him of a story that my father told back in the sixties. A man who was stricken with lockjaw was taken to the hospital for treatment. The doctor advised, "Give him a little whiskey." In order to administer the liquor, it was necessary to bore a hole through a tooth and inject it through a funnel. It had a stimulating effect; the patient was aroused and making his voice heard through his closed teeth begged them to funnel him again.

I remember one day my mother told a story that was recalled by the charitable attitude of a visitor. It reminded her of another woman so kindly in her treatment of others that she never could bear to have anybody criticized in her presence. One day the children conspired together to see how far the mother could carry her charity. They assembled one by one in her room and began to criticize the devil just to see if their mother would take his part. They had not proceeded far when the mother interrupted them with the admonition, "Well, children, if we were all as industrious as the devil is, we would all accomplish more."

After the children were grown and the three older ones had established homes of their own, mother moved from the farm into Salem. I had then prospered sufficiently to be able to buy her a home near to the home of my oldest sister, and I never spent money that brought me more real pleasure.

In the fall of 1895, she was stricken down with an illness that resulted fatally the following June. I shall never forget her last Christmas with us. We took the children (Ruth was about ten, William six, and Grace four) with us to spend the holidays at Salem. Four of her five children were there and five grandchildren also. Mother sat up in bed and distributed the presents. I never saw her happier; her cheerfulness enlivened our Christmas reunion and is a cherished recollection.

She died ten days before my nomination for the presidency. I went from her funeral to the Chicago convention. Often I have thought of the joy it would have given her if she could have lived to see me nominated. And then I check the thought, for in her weakened condition the excitement might have been too much for her. The fact that she was not spared to share in the proud satisfaction that my nomination brought to the family made me glad that the mother of my successful rival lived to see her son in the White House. A mother's pride is so genuine and so excusable that we forget political differences as we are united in a common humanity.

Such were the parents to whom, and such was the home in which I was born.

My name was drawn from the two families that were united by the marriage of my parents. William was a family name with the Bryans; the name of my father's oldest brother and the name of their grandfather. Jennings was my mother's maiden name. A few years ago I met a

man in Missouri who was a little more than a hundred years
old. He had lived in Marion County at the time of my
birth. In the conversation that I had with him, he claimed
credit for having suggested my name. He said that my
father wanted to name me William and that my mother
desired me to bear the name Jennings. He made the quite
natural suggestion that both names be given to me, and so
it was. In my youth my name went through all the forms
of which it was capable; like the boy of whom James Whit-
comb Riley writes,

> "Father calls me William,
>   And mother calls me Will;
> Sister calls me Billy,
>   But the fellers call me Bill."

Possibly Willy was more frequently used by my mother
and brothers and sisters during the early years, while Will
became my settled name as I advanced from boyhood into
young manhood.

In the spring of 1866 my father decided to move to the
country, the reason being that he thought a farm a better
place to raise a family. There were three of us at that time,
Russell Jones, Frances Mariah, and myself. The site selected
was about a mile northwest from the center of Salem—that
is, a mile by the road, although not quite so far in a direct
line. There were two ways of going out to the place. The
Prairie Road way, as we used to call it, took us half a mile
west of the square and then a mile north; or the Woods
Road that turned to the north about a quarter of a mile
from the square and passed through the strip of woods.
The house stood in a level piece of land, approached from
the east by an avenue a quarter mile long and leading up to
what seemed to me quite an elevation. It was not more
than twenty or twenty-five feet, and as I have revisited the
place in later years I wondered how the hill could have

seemed so high. Perhaps it is due to the magnifying power of time, for all the hills in the neighborhood have shrunk, and the streams that seemed deep appear shallow.

The house was of brick and faced to the east and had a porch set in on the front and back side of the main living room. It was of the style quite familiar in Virginia, with a hall running through the center.

A commodious yard about three hundred feet long and two hundred feet wide contained a row of cedars on each side of the walk and several rows of maples. I still measure distances by the distances that I learned to know in this country home. A hundred yards is still the distance between our front door and the gate, a quarter mile is the length of the avenue, and the half mile is the distance from our farm fence to the main street.

My father used to take me out to the farm while the house was being built and the workmen allowed me to help to the limit of my small ability. I would carry a brick on a shingle and in my boyish pride felt that I was having a part in the construction of the building that was to be my home for seventeen years.

A piano was the principal piece of furniture in the parlor and is often recalled. One of the pictures most clearly outlined in my memory is the picture of the family gathered in this room on Sunday afternoon, singing Sunday-school songs and church hymns. Mother played the accompaniment and led in the singing. The Bryan Choir, as father called it, joined with youthful enthusiasm. Father's favorite piece was "Kind Words" and we were wont to close the singing with his favorite song. To these Sunday afternoon exercises, as well as to the Sunday school, I am indebted for these tunes that have run through my mind ever since.

The spare bedroom was set apart for the special entertainment of politicians and divines. The bringing together of these two classes illustrated not only my father's views on the subjects but early taught me to regard the science

33

of government as an entirely honorable one. My father was as much at home with ministers as he was with politicians and statesmen. He saw no necessary conflict—and I have never been able to see any—between the principles of our government and the principles of Christian faith.

One of the pieces of furniture of that day which seems to have disappeared in modern times was the trundle bed. It enabled the younger children to sleep in the same room with their parents and at the same time space in the room to be utilized in the daytime.

Our farm contained five hundred twenty acres in one block, nearly all of it prairie, with a small woods pasture near and an eighty-acre piece of timber about three miles away. We had a park of fourteen acres adjoining the farm where my father indulged his fancy for deer, the number running up at times as high as twenty. We had the usual farm animals, horses, cattle, hogs, sheep, and, of course, the usual supply of poultry which included turkeys, guineas, and ducks as well as chickens. As I look back upon those days, I feel a little disappointed that we did not have geese, fowls that I used to associate with the family visits which we made to our grandparents, who lived near Walnut Hill, Illinois, about twelve miles away. There was a creek in front of the house and the geese that frequented it, always on the lookout, gave their noisy warning at our approach.

My parents were not fanciers of pure-bred stock, although I remember several excellent males that were bought from time to time, as a bull to which we gave the name "White Cloud" which was sent to us from Jacksonville—he was a gift from Dr. Jones, whose name will become familiar to the readers of these memoirs. I remember that we were very proud of him until he became vicious, when we had to dispose of him. My first experience with pigs was with a Chester White boar. I took him to the fair one fall, and have a very distinct recollection of the amount of washing necessary to keep a white pig clean.

IN THE BEGINNING

As we rented the land out and cultivated only a few acres, our place might have better been called a suburban home than a farm, but we had enough farm life to give us experience as children. The boys had the wood to cut and the chores to do. I, being the oldest, used the laboring oar, so to speak, and learned to milk and care for the stock and to do the general chores. If I were required to select the days of my boyhood which were least enjoyed the lot would fall on the winter days of this period. My first business was to make the fire in the Franklin stove and then go to the barn and feed the horses, cows, and hogs. Then came the milking and then breakfast. Sometimes we had a farm hand and I played the part of assistant, but much of the time we did not have enough work to justify the employment of a man in the winter time and the burden fell on me.

More than fifty years have passed since those days and I can see myself engaged in this drudgery, my nose running, my fingers numb, and possessing feelings for which the Sunday-school songs I knew did not furnish fitting expression. And yet, I look back to those days as among the most valuable of my life and I would not for anything have them eliminated. They taught me industry and obedience and they gave me an exercise which no gymnasium can supply. My physical strength has been an invaluable asset and I feel that I am indebted to work upon the farm for the strength that has enabled me to endure fatigue and withstand disease. Our verdicts which we pronounce in youth are often reviewed and set aside in mature life. I am sure that the indictments which I would have framed about the time the chores were done are very unlike the judgments that I now render in retrospect.

Rabbit Hunting

My favorite sport in those early days was hunting rabbits. My father had something of the spirit of the hunter. I presume it came down in his blood from a Virginia

35

ancestry. At any rate, he used to take me out squirrel hunting and I was all interest from the time we began to prepare for the hunt, moulding the bullets the night before for a muzzle-loading rifle, to the time when we came back with one or possibly two squirrels as a reward for an afternoon's tramp. But while I envied my father's skill as a marksman, I never attempted to rival him with the rifle. I began with a shotgun, first with a single barrel and then with a double barrel. These were given to me as soon as my parents thought it was entirely safe for me to use them, possibly a little earlier than it was entirely safe, for I remember three narrow escapes from death by gunshot.

One day I was cleaning the gun in the hallway and it went off, blowing a hole through the baseboard, but I was not in front of it at the time. It scared me and I was careful, but not, I fear, as careful as I should have been. A little later I was putting a double barreled shotgun through a rail fence and foolishly had the barrel pointed toward me. The hammer struck a rail and discharged the cap—but fortunately, the gun did not go off. I could not have escaped death if the fire of the cap had reached the powder. Why it did not, I do not know, for that was its only failure to fire during the hunt.

At another time Henry Webster, my nearest neighbor, went with me out to Tonti, the nearest station on the Illinois Central, to meet my father, who was returning from holding court in one of the courts of his circuit. We got out at a pond near the road to shoot some snipe. I suppose we must have forgotten to let down the hammer. At any rate, the gun that was between us went off and blew a hole through the back curtain. We were singing "O, you must be a lover of the Lord, or you can't go to heaven when you die." Our musical program was suspended by the discharge of the gun and we rode the rest of the way exchanging congratulations upon our escape and wondering how the gun could have discharged.

36

IN THE BEGINNING

Before I was old enough to use a gun I used to hunt rabbits with a stick, tracking them in the snow and killing them in the little sheltered spots so familiar to hunters of this familiar game.

I had two dogs, Carlo and Dixie, the latter a mixed breed with rat terrier predominating. Carlo was a dog of medium size. If any one pure strain could be multiplied by the many strains mixed in him, he would have been a very costly brute. But as prices are not determined in this way, he would have brought at auction as little as he cost me— nothing. The dogs hunted together, Dixie would go in under the brush piles and scare the rabbits out and Carlo jumped stiff legged around the pile and would take up the chase as soon as the frightened rabbit came out. I followed the dogs, scrambling over fences, helping to pick up the trail when there was snow on the ground, and returning as jubilant in defeat as in victory. Many times when I almost froze during the chores I would warm myself by a chase after a rabbit until all the hardships of work were forgotten. After I began going to school, a part of each Saturday was given over to some kind of sport, usually a rabbit hunt, and one rabbit seemed to be my normal luck, although sometimes I would come back with several.

At times I would get my first game soon after I started and carry it for several hours and sometimes I would trudge along without reward until nearly home and then unexpectedly catch a rabbit. We had a boardwalk which ran diagonally from the front porch to the garden gate and intersected the walk from the kitchen to the barn. As the boards were nailed crosswise on two by fours, the walk furnished a splendid hiding place for rabbits and it trapped many for me.

As I grew older I extended my hunting to quail, prairie chickens, and ducks. The quail, however, was never much endangered by my hunting. It seemed too small for my gun and I was frequently mortified by having a hunting companion give me the first shot and then kill the bird after I had missed it.

With prairie chickens I had better success. Probably they furnished a larger target, but even here I was only a second-rate hunter. One time, I think it was in 1897, I went hunting in Idaho with the father of the famous Chicago lawyer, A. S. Trude. I think he was then about eighty. He had lost one eye, which to a hunter is quite a disadvantage. When we came in from the most successful chicken hunt I ever had we counted up thirty fowls and he was generous enough to insist that I had killed ten of them—half as many as he. I used to wonder what the relative success would have been if he had had two eyes.

Soon after the election of 1896 I became acquainted with William L. Moody, a prominent banker of Galveston. Governor Hogg, his attorney, made me acquainted with him and established him in my affections by telling me that he was the only prominent banker in Galveston who voted for me. When Governor Hogg was describing a hunt he gave a very vivid picture of the hunting at Lake Surprise. Three items of his description are recalled. The first was that you could hunt ducks there in a dress suit, and this I found to be true. We were entertained at a commodious house near the lake, where we had comfortable beds and the best of food. A spring wagon would take us to the lake, where we entered canoes and rowed to the blinds which were hidden in reedy islands in the lake. Here we would sit and shoot until our hunting hour was over. Then boatmen would gather up the ducks, carry us back to the landing place, from which the spring wagon would carry us back to the house. There was nothing to soil one's evening dress had he cared so to clothe himself. On one of my visits I took Mrs. Bryan with me and she sat in the blind and read to me while I waited for the waterfowl to appear. Another item in his description was that the ducks were so numerous that the noise made by their feet in the celery in the lake sounded like the roar of a train and that the noise made by their flying was like the rumbling of distant thunder. These accounts seem quite extravagant, but they were true to the letter. I have never found anywhere such hunting places as Colonel Moody used to furnish at Lake Surprise and never a more genial and hospitable host than Colonel Moody, whose son J. L. or his younger son, Henry, or his son-in-law, Northen, expert with the gun, went with us.

Our trips usually extended from the evening of the first day through the morning and evening of the second day and the morning of the third day. When I first went down there I was inclined to joke about the game law, saying that a law limiting each person to twenty-five ducks a day was never intended for me because I did not expect to come near the limit, and that a law prohibiting more than twenty-five shots at one duck might have been *more* embarrassing to me. But on a later visit, just before a hotel temporarily destroyed the value of the lake as a hunting resort, I had a streak of luck. I killed my quota of twenty-five before sundown on the first afternoon and then killed my quota the morning of the next day so that in the afternoon I had to content myself with pointing out ducks to others. Next morning I again killed my quota before noon, making seventy-five for the three days. This was my record day, surpassing all other hunting experiences.

My father was in the habit of impressing his views upon me by apt illustrations or humor. I recall that during my early boyhood I expressed a desire to take lessons on the piano. He checked my ambitions in this direction with the brief but firm suggestion that the girls in the family could take lessons on the piano but that the boys would learn to make music with the hand saw. I have only inherited half of his views on this subject. When I hear a song that appeals to my heart I envy those who are able to sing. But experience has confirmed in me the views of my father about music in general. One has only so much

39

time. If it is spent on instrumental music sufficient to become proficient it occupies time that must be taken from other things, as for instance, reading, from which I think more practical value is derived. It is a very pleasant thing for a man to be able to furnish music to a company, but it is sometimes done at the expense of other lines of development. If one cannot reach the maximum in both entertainment and service, service is the more important of the two.

My parents believed in the old adage, "Spare the rod and spoil the child," and as they loved me too well to risk my being spoiled, they punished me. As I look back upon these punishments, I find myself more tolerant in passing judgment upon them than I was at the time, although I recall instances where I recognized the punishment as just, and some instances where I felt that I deserved more than I received. They were quite strict with me and I sometimes considered the boys more fortunate who were given more liberty, but on reflection I am not prepared to say that I would have done better under a different system. Other kinds of discipline may be better for other children—that parents must decide for themselves. I am not only satisfied but grateful for the punishment I received.

At the age of ten I was sent to school; before that time my mother taught me at home. Grandma's room—the back sitting room—was my first schoolhouse, and a little walnut table about two feet square, as my memory reproduces it today, was the first stump from which I made a speech. I would learn my lessons until I could repeat questions and answers without the book and then I would stand up on this little table and declaim them to my mother. My first audience, therefore, was a receptive, appreciative, and enthusiastic one.

Webster's spelling book and McGuffey's reader, then a geography, whose author I cannot recall, formed the basis of my education and furnished the themes for my earliest

40

declamations. I would like to own this table, but it has thus far eluded my search.

A difference of opinion may arise as to the inheritance of my ability as a speaker. My father's talent in this line of work may form the basis for argument in support of hereditary ability, but I am inclined to give more weight to environment than to inheritance. It is unusual for the descendants of a prominent public speaker to excel in speaking, and differences among those who inherit equally would seem to raise a doubt as to the value of ancestral abilities. The child of a public speaker has the influence of his father's example and the inspiration that comes from an ambition to be like him. If to this is added the devotion and diligence of a mother who, like my mother, encouraged the tendency, the weight of the argument may be on the side of environment rather than heredity.

I began very young to manifest an interest in speaking and received all the encouragement that a child could from both father and mother. As the profession which I liked leads up to forensic efforts, it must also be taken into consideration no child could have had an environment more favorable to a public career or stronger incentives to follow this particular line of work. As the story proceeds illustrations will be given of the continuity of purpose and the permanence of the ambition.

In School

The first public school I attended was in what we called "The Old College," a building once used for a girls' seminary. When the school was abandoned the building was turned over to the city and my first lessons from a teacher of a public school were given me there.

Mrs. Lamb was the teacher, a woman somewhat advanced in years at that time but an enthusiast on education and a strict disciplinarian.

I next attended a school in a different part of the town

41

and soon entered the high school, from which I went to Whipple Academy, a preparatory department of Illinois College, Jacksonville.

During these five years in the public school I do not recall much that is worth recording. I walked in to school, a distance of three-quarters of a mile to the first building and about a mile to the second and to the high school. I was regular in attendance and studious, having behind me the coercive power of parents who were determined that I should have an education. I do not recall that I ever failed in an examination, neither do I remember to have been at the head of the class in these earlier days. I might have been called an average—I was not below the average in my studies and well toward the front in deportment. In the high school I began studying Latin and also went a step forward in the art of declamation in the literary society work. We had a debating club in the high school and I recall taking a part in what we called The Senate, and I was a senator from Illinois. It may have been that this experience in a "senate" suggested to me the thought of being some time a Senator of the United States. This ambition received encouragement from my father's race for Congress in 1872 when I was twelve years old.

I early became interested in the political news in the papers and recall very distinctly the eagerness with which I searched the columns of the *Missouri Republican*, the first prominent political newspaper I ever read.

I do not remember the subjects debated, but I recall that in one debate in which the color question came up, I used a sentence which brought forth applause when in the course of a brief speech I described something under consideration as "the darkest picture ever painted upon the canvas of time."

It was during my high-school days that I made my first venture in poetry, but while the jingle was praised by the schoolmates who saw it, the success

42

was not sufficient to turn my head or my mind in that direction.

My father, being a very devout man, lost no opportunity to impress upon me the value of the Bible. To him it was not only the Word of God but the fountain of wisdom. He was especially fond of Proverbs and was in the habit of calling me in from work a little before noon to read a chapter and comment upon it. I cannot say that I shared his enthusiasm at the time—in fact, I was at times a little restless and even wished that I might have been allowed to devote the time to work in the field rather than to the reading and comment. But when he died, soon after I was twenty, the Biblical truths that he sought to impress upon me grew in value and I took up the book of Proverbs and read it through once a month for a year. I have frequently mentioned this experience and advised young men to read Proverbs because of the accumulated wisdom to be found therein—wisdom on all moral questions and expressed with wonderful force and clearness. I have quoted from Proverbs in my political speeches more than from any other part of the Bible or from any other book. Solomon left a rare collection of epigrams and it was the reading of Proverbs that gave me my first appreciation of the value of epigram.

The moulding of public opinion is one of the greatest of the arts, and the essence of moulding public opinion lies in the ability to say much in a few words. No uninspired writer has left so much of wisdom contained in so small a compass. One of the proverbs of Solomon which I early learned and often quoted was "A prudent man forseeth the evil, and hideth himself." This cannot be improved upon so far as the sentiment is concerned or the beauty of expression, but I found that audiences—especially students —did not seem to grasp it. As the object of speaking is to impress truth, I finally took the liberty of presenting this truth in a way most familiar to the student and most easily remembered. The paraphrase ran like this, "The prudent man gets the idea into his head, the foolish man 'gets it in the neck.'" The students instantly caught the idea and I felt that the impressing of the idea did more good than the slang did harm. The consolation of the reformer is that if he is right in uttering the warning and the people do not heed, they will come to him when their necks are sore.

My religious training was not neglected at any period of my life. We had family prayers—one of the sweetest recollections of my boyhood days—and I entered Sunday school early. My father being a Baptist and my mother being a Methodist, I went to both Sunday schools. The only advantage that I know of that can come from the parents belonging to the different churches is that the Sunday-school opportunities are doubled. I would not offer this as sufficient reason for encouraging a difference in church membership on the part of parents, but where there is a difference of this kind, the Sunday school may, to some extent, be an off-setting advantage—at least, in my case it gave to me the double interest in Sunday-school work, an interest which has never waned.

At the age of fourteen I reached one of the turning points in my life. I attended a revival that was being conducted in a Presbyterian church and was converted. Having been brought up in a Christian home, conversion did not mean a change in my habits of life or habits of thought. I do not know of a virtue that came into my life as a result of my joining the Church, because all the virtues had been taught me by my parents. Truthfulness had been so earnestly enjoined that in more than one case I received my parents' commendation for not misrepresenting the situation when truthfulness might bring criticism if not punishment.

I remember that one day we children were playing in the sitting room, and noticing father's pocketbook upon the bureau, it occurred to some one of us—I do not know which—to count the money, so we locked the door and proceeded to inform ourselves upon the amount in the pocketbook. When we were just finishing we heard his footfall in the hall. We hurriedly crowded the money into the pocketbook and opened the door, but not soon enough to avoid suspicion. When he found me alone he asked me what we were doing. I told him we were counting his money, whereupon he took me down town and bought me a saddle, presenting it and telling me, as he presented it, to remember I received it for telling the truth. I do not know of any similar amount of money that ever made so great an impression upon my youthful mind and heart.

As an illustration of the teaching which I received at home I cite two other instances. Before entering school at the age of ten my mother so impressed upon me her opinion of swearing—a matter in which my father also set me a valuable example—that when I entered school I felt a distinct aversion to swearing. I would find myself withdrawing from the crowd when the boys began to swear, and to this day I have not overcome an aversion which I felt in those early days.

The other subject impressed on me was that it was wrong to gamble. My father hated gambling and taught me to hate it. With him it did not matter whether the amount wagered was large or small or whether the person won or lost—gambling was gambling. Some time before I was fifteen I had an experience that almost rivaled the gift of the saddle in the impression it made. My father had bought me a forty-cent knife which I wagered against a ten-cent knife on a proposition where I felt that I could not lose. The boys had given me a number of cards, each containing a series of numbers. These numbers were so arranged that the sum of the first numbers on each card equaled the number asked for. After I had used the cards until I felt confident of their accuracy, I undertook to tell the age of a boy's mother if he would pick out the cards on

45

which the age appeared. The wager was my knife against his and I lost. Upon examination, I found that the number required was the only one which could not be determined by the adding together of the first numbers on the cards containing this number. Knowing my father's views on gambling, I was so terrified at the thought of his learning what I had done that I resolved never to gamble again, no matter how certain I might be to win. The loss of a forty-cent knife has saved me a great deal of money, if I can judge what my experience would have been from the experiences of friends who have bet on elections where I, like they, thought the result was certain.

CHAPTER II

CHURCH AND SCHOOL

IN becoming a member of the Church I entered upon an important epoch—much more important than I thought at the time. I was, of course, too young to know anything about the creeds of the different churches. I knew the names of the churches and had attended all of them at different times and had been connected with the Sunday schools of several of them. The Baptist Church in Salem had a very small congregation at that time. There was preaching there once a month and but very few young people in the Sunday school. The Methodist Church was a larger organization and I went to the Baptist Sunday school in the morning and the Methodist Sunday school in the afternoon. Besides these denominations the Presbyterian and Cumberland Presbyterian and the Catholics had congregations there. The last named ministered to but a few families. After my mother joined the Baptist Church with my father, about 1872, I began to attend the Cumberland Presbyterian Church in the afternoon. It had one of the largest congregations in the city and a great many children in that church were my companions in school. I think no other Sunday school had so large an influence upon my life.

The superintendent was the best Sunday-school superintendent I have ever known—at least, he so seems to me as I look back through the years and recall his devotion to the school, his friendly attitude toward all the children, and our intimate acquaintance with him. He seemed like one of the family; we liked to meet him on the street and enjoyed being sent to his store to make purchases. He was always on hand and the lessons that he drew from the Bible text are yet part of our thoughts and lives. If in the world beyond, he knows, as I believe he does, how affectionately the children remember him, it will be abundant reward for the time he devoted to his work—probably he felt that he received his reward as he went along from a consciousness of service rendered and from the knowledge of the affectionate regard the children had for him.

Then there was Sam Chance, who led the singing. He had one of the sweetest tenor voices I have ever heard; his notes still ring in my ears. He has only one rival among those nonprofessionals to whom I have listened. My wife's father had a tenor voice, not so strong as Mr. Chance's but fully as sweet and as expressive, but I did not hear him until considerably later in life—and then I heard him sing frequently.

There is one fact in connection with my early days that should, I think, be recorded, namely, my parents' willingness to allow me to choose at that early age a church different from their own. It was an evidence of their liberality in denominational matters, notwithstanding the deep and permanent convictions which they had on Christian fundamentals. I noted this liberality first in the attitude of each in the other's church before they became members of the same church. I noticed it also in their treatment of ministers of the various churches who were occasionally assembled at our house at family dinner. I was also impressed by the fact that when we gathered our hay my father was in habit of sending a load away to each minister, including the Catholic priest when a priest resided there.

This liberality was also proof of the deep concern about my religious life. When I asked my father whether he had any objections to my joining the Presbyterian Church— my inclination to join being based upon two facts: first, my conversion at a revival held in that Church; and second being the fact that some seventy young people of the Sunday school, my schoolmates in the day school, joined at that time—he said that he wanted me to join where I felt

I would be most at home and could do the most good. I never knew until after his death that he was disappointed that I did not become a member of his own church.

When, a year later, I entered Whipple Academy at Jacksonville, I took my letter to the Presbyterian Church at Jacksonville and remained a member of it until 1887, when I took my letter to the First Presbyterian Church at Lincoln, Nebraska. Though my connection with the Presbyterian Church at Salem was very brief, the church has had a very warm place in my heart for half a century. Six years ago I presented to the church a pulpit made after a pattern which appealed to me at Dr. Hindman's church, the Northminster Presbyterian Church at Columbus, Ohio. The pulpit was made for him by an elder whose father was an elder in the Presbyterian Church in Scotland.

In front of the pulpit was a cross and in the center was a burning bush—the cross representative of the New Testament and the bush the Old Testament. This so deeply impressed me that I had a replica of the Columbus pulpit made for the church at Salem. I spoke at its dedication in May, 1920, my subject being "Symbols of Service." Dr. Glover, pastor of the Jacksonville Church when I became a member of it, was a man who had ministered to the church for a generation. He became my personal friend as well as my pastor and I feel that he exerted a very beneficial influence on my life at that formative period. His wife, who shared in his devotion to spiritual things, invited me to her home one evening that she might appeal to me to prepare for the ministry. While I had great regard for the ministry, I did not feel that my life work lay along that line and, therefore, while I was willing to hear what she had to say, I was prepared to defend my choice of the law as a life pursuit. I recall that I had fortified myself with the third verse of the twenty-first chapter of Proverbs: "To do justice and judgment is more acceptable to the Lord than sacrifice." When I called at her home I found that sickness of a relative had taken her away from town and, as the invitation was not renewed, I never had occasion to weigh the reasons that she had intended to present.

After Dr. Glover's death, which was before my graduation, Dr. J. R. Southerland was called to the church and the attachment formed between us continued until his death a few years ago. He was succeeded by A. B. Morey. Although his pastorate was brief, it was long enough to become the basis of an attachment between us that lasted till his recent death. His successor had a personality and charm that made a deep impression on me. In one sermon he gave a graphic picture of the right way and the wrong way of doing a thing. He said that to take a tree through a little gate you must take the trunk first, then the limbs would be pressed in against the trunk. If, on the contrary, he attempted to take it through by pulling the limbs through first, the other limbs would catch against the gatepost and prevent progress.

When in 1887 we moved to Nebraska we found Dr. Curtis pastor of the First Presbyterian Church. He was called to a Chicago church and was followed by Dr. Hindman, with whom I became intimately associated, and this friendship I have cherished through years that have followed. Dr. Henry V. Swearingen, who was later Moderator, followed Dr. Hindman. He, too, became one of the inner circle of our friends.

Soon after moving to our country place, Fairview, near Lincoln, Nebraska, in 1902 we took our letters to the Westminster Presbyterian Church. I was elected elder of this church and held the position until we took our letters to the First Presbyterian Church of Miami, Florida, in 1921. But in order that we might know our neighbors better we attended the Methodist Church in Normal. In the Sunday school Mrs. Bryan assisted as teacher, and I was a teacher from time to time as my traveling would permit.

As I look back over the years, I am increasingly grateful

for the religious environment that surrounded me in my youth and the devotion of my parents and for the influence that the Church had upon me in my school days. The period through which one passes in the journey from youth to maturity is quite likely to be accompanied by some religious uncertainty. In the course of nature the child will substitute the spirit of independence for the spirit of dependence. Instead of doing things because he is told to, he must do them upon his own responsibility and from his own convictions. During this transition period the pendulum is apt to swing too far and he sometimes finds himself more self-reliant than he ought to be and less disposed to be influenced by advice of others. It is just at this time when the parental authority is weakening that usually the student begins in the study of the physical sciences. If he is fortunate enough to have teachers who are themselves Christians with a spiritual vision of life, the effect is to strengthen his faith and he advances to a normal religious life. If he is unfortunate enough to fall under the influence of mind worshipers, he may be led step by step away from faith into unbelief. It is a matter of profound gratitude to me that during these days I was associated with Christian instructors so that the doubts aroused by my studies were resolved by putting them beside a powerful and loving God. Knowledge of the experiences of students has made me very sympathetic with students in college and has led me to go from college to college in the hope of helping young men to find solid ground upon which to stand. It was this interest in young men more than anything else which led me to prepare and deliver the address entitled, "The Prince of Peace." (See Chapter XXI.)

Whipple Academy

At the academy I got my first taste of college life. It looked a long road ahead of me when I counted up the two years at the academy and the four years at the college before the day of graduation. And it was the classical course, too. I cannot remember when I decided to go to college—in fact, I do not recall that I ever did decide to go to college. It was decided for me by my parents and when I was too young to fix the day. All I know is that I was going to college from my earliest recollection. I was not only going to college but I was going to take the highest course the college provided, and the plan was later elaborated by the addition of a post-graduate course at Oxford, England. My father was enthused upon the subject of education and my mother fully shared with him this desire for the children. When not long before his death I sat by his bedside and in the presence of my mother took down at his dictation the words of his will, he expressed in a paragraph this ideal which had led him as a poor boy to make a successful struggle for a classical education. He directed that all of the children (I was then twenty and there were four younger than myself) should have the best education that the generation afforded. Not long before he died he bought fifty calves which were to grow until I graduated at Illinois College and then were to be turned into money, the money to be used for a year at Oxford. It so happened that when he died he owed security debts to the amount of about $15,000, the larger part represented by a note given by a man to his sister which father endorsed. In settling up the estate it seemed best to sell the cattle and pay off those security debts, so that my trip to Europe was given up. My mother took enough of the calf money to purchase for me a gold watch which I carried until it was replaced by the precious timepiece given me by the employees in the State Department.

In September after my fifteenth anniversary I was sent to Whipple Academy, Jacksonville, a preparatory school connected with Illinois College. Here again I was the beneficiary of one of the best bits of good fortune that has fallen to my lot. My father, being a Baptist, had intended to send me to William Jewell College in Liberty, Missouri, an institution of his own denomination which he had come to hold in high esteem. If I had been two or three years older I presume he would have carried out this purpose and I would have been brought into contact with other personalities and my life might have been moulded by an entirely different chain of circumstances. My father had a distant relative, a physician of prominence, Dr. Hiram K. Jones, between whom and my father a warm friendship had developed. Dr. Jones was a man of the highest character, of great learning, and lofty ideals. His wife, Cousin Lizzie, as we called her, was one of the sweetest characters which it has ever been my privilege to know. She was a woman of rare intelligence, fond of literature and music, and was possessed of temper that nothing could ruffle. She was so charitable in her attitude toward others that I do not recall having heard her say an unkind word of anyone during the six years that I made my home in the family. Even a criticism made by others would pain her as if it were directed against her and she would protest with a sincerity that was manifested in both tone of voice and in the expression of pain upon her face.

Dr. Jones was the head of the literary circle of the city and for some years a lecturer at the Concord (Massachusetts) School of Philosophy. His specialty was Plato. Possibly no scholar of his day was more thoroughly acquainted with the work of the great Greek philosopher. Dr. Jones' diversion was microscopy and he often called me in to examine the specimens upon which he was working.

Dr. and Mrs. Jones were members of the Congregational Church and he was a trustee of Illinois College, which was founded by a group of Yale graduates who came out to Jacksonville in the early years of the century. As I view in retrospect my own life in the Jones family I find it difficult to calculate the influence which association with them had upon my ideas and ideals. They had no children and

WILLIAM JENNINGS BRYAN

I was only one of a number of schoolboys to whom they had furnished a home, and these, as I came to know them, were as grateful as I became for the splendid environment furnished.

Dr. H. K. Jones had a brother, Dr. George Jones, ten years his junior, who was associated in the practice with him. He was a man of different type but one to whom I became also attached. His wife, an admirable woman, was more or less of an invalid. Their house was in the same yard as that of the elder doctor, so that my acquaintance with them was almost as intimate as with Dr. and Mrs. H. K. Jones. The families furnished a splendid illustration of the strength and tenderness of family ties. Dr. George and his wife had no children and, like the family with whom I made my home, they nearly always had students with them. These were my most intimate friends during these delightful days.

I began Greek in my first preparatory year and Latin in the second year. Like most boys, I was relatively further along in mathematics than in the languages.

When I left home for school father told me that he was able to furnish me with the money that I actually needed but that he could not afford to have me waste money, and then he suggested what I have always believed to be a good rule, that I should keep an account and report to him the use I had already made of the money when I wrote for more. This I proceeded to do and I do not recall that he ever referred to the expenditures except in one case.

I had spent ten cents for blacking, twenty cents for bay rum, and ten cents for candy. I entered the account as "forty cents for blacking, bay rum, etc.," the "etc." covering the candy. It so happened that the next entry was "to the church, five cents." He sent me the money that I asked for, merely adding by way of comment, "I notice that you spent forty cents for blacking and five cents for the church. It seems to me that that is travelling toward

54

the Dead Sea pretty fast." I can imagine that there was a smile upon his face when he wrote this reproof, but it answered the purpose. I never covered any expenditures afterward with "etc." and I never forgot the inference that he drew from the relative size of the amount spent for improvement of my appearance and the amount spent for the church.

I hope that it will not seem to the reader too trivial if I add that this old account book fell into my wife's hands after we were married and she discovered that the first item of my college account was "five cents for a bologna sausage," spelled "ballony." Another entry was, "oysters and needles—15c."

When I first left home I was growing very rapidly. I have reason to remember, because I wrote back home for money to buy a new pair of pants, explaining to my father that my pants had become so short that I was ashamed to attend the church sociables. He wrote back saying that I would soon be home for the holidays and could then replenish my wardrobe and added, "But you might as well learn now that people will measure you by the length of your head and not by the length of your breeches."

College Years

By the fall of 1877 I entered college proper. While I was only a freshman, the two years' experience in the academy had somewhat worn off my freshness and I felt well on the road toward manhood. I had developed so rapidly during the years preceding that I had almost reached my growth. My ambition was to be six feet in height and weigh 180. That was my idea of the proper height and weight; possibly I had obtained my standard of height from my father who was a little more than six feet tall. He did not, however, give me my idea of weight, because he weighed only 154, as I had reason to know.

When I went home from college for a vacation we happened to weigh at the same time. He weighed 154 and I weighed 150. I was rather proud of my weight and said, "I shall soon be as heavy as you are." He replied with a twinkle of the eye, "When you have four pounds more of brains we will weigh the same." The next time we weighed I weighed more than he did and recalling his remark I attributed all the increase as "brain weight."

I did not give much attention to athletics during college. My principal exercise was walking from my boarding place on College Avenue up to my recitations and back and down town and back, as I had frequent occasions to run errands for Dr. or Mrs. Jones. While I played games to some extent, I was not an expert except at jumping. When I played baseball I was usually assigned to the right field, where my inefficiency would least embarrass the club. In my younger days I had been more conspicuous upon the diamond, but my prestige waned when the round bat was substituted for the flat bat and when the ball began to be thrown instead of pitched. The curve was always a mystery to me and I never secured sufficient control of the muscles of my face to restrain the expression of surprise called forth by the curved balls that passed me unimpeded in their flight. But when it came to the broad jump I had to be reckoned with. I was somewhat proficient in the running broad jump, but the only thing in which I excelled was what we used to call the standing jump, known technically, I believe, as the standing broad jump. I began at nine feet when I entered the academy. I gradually increased the distance until I won a prize with a record of twelve feet four inches. I would commence jumping as soon as the frost was out of the ground and jump until I was sore and then I would continue jumping until the soreness disappeared.

I entered many jumping contests, but one competitor after another fell behind. I remember one good-natured rival, Charlie Carter, who, when he discovered that his efforts were hopeless, vented his disappointment in the following good-natured rebuke: "Bryan, my father always told me never to speak of anyone unless I could speak well of him. Whenever I speak of you I always say you are a good jumper." I have thought of this many times since when a stranger introducing himself would say, "Mr. Bryan, I must say that you are a man of wonderful physical endurance." I know by that compliment that he is a Republican, he wants to speak kindly and he can say this much without making any political concessions.

My practice in the jumping forward led me also to practice the jump backwards, in which I left a record of nine feet. I do not recall but one man who surpassed me in the jump backward. There is more of art than strength in this jump, a good deal depending upon so balancing as to use the weight of the body without being thrown off one's feet. Very few can jump any considerable distance backward and the number of those who can jump three jumps backward without falling is still less.

I did not have much chance to hunt while I was in college, although occasionally when there was snow on the ground I went out on Saturday with a college friend. I remember one of these hunts with Oscar Kenneth, one of the members of the class who unfortunately died soon after graduation. We started out early in the morning and hunted until late in the afternoon. The dinner that his mother served to us about four o'clock stands out in my memory as one of the most refreshing meals in my life. It was not that there was great variety of unusual food, but there was plenty and we were hungry—the two necessary elements of a satisfying meal.

I early became acquainted with Glenn Hulett and was frequently his guest. He lives a few miles in the country and we became a terror to the rabbits in the neighborhood. I devote more space to this friend when I speak of my college course. We were rivals and our marks were quite close together at the end of four years' race. But one of the most delightful of rivalries it was. Our friendship was never disturbed by our ambitions. I would have congratulated him as heartily as he did me; if he had been the victor I would have felt that it was an honor to be next to him.

I took the classical course, not as a matter of choice, because I had no choice in the matter. My father and mother decided that question and told me what I was to do, as they had decided for me the question of going to college. I do not know the date of the decision; I only know that from my earliest recollection I was going to college and was going to take the highest course. When I left home, father took from his library two of the largest books, a Greek lexicon and a Latin lexicon, and told me that I was to use the former for six years in the study of Greek and the latter five years in the study of Latin. I did not then know of their importance, but have since been very glad that there were others wiser than myself to decide such questions for me. I have come to place a high estimate upon the study of the dead languages because of the training they give one in the choice of words and because of the acquaintance that they give the student with the derivation of words. I liked Latin better than the Greek—possibly because it is easier. I became so attached to the Latin that I planned to read some Latin every year as a recreation. But I soon became so occupied with work which was necessary that the sentimental was crowded out.

Mathematics was my favorite study until I took up political economy. During the senior year of my preparatory work I took freshman college mathematics and was marked one hundred in geometry. I was a contestant for the freshman prize in mathematics with Sam Montgomery, a boy who was taking the scientific course. I do not know which had the highest marks, because I learned before the prize was awarded that the competition was open only to those who were in the freshman class. This excluded me.

THE COLLEGE LITERARY SOCIETIES

Students of Whipple Academy were permitted to enter the literary societies of the college and I immediately availed myself of this opportunity, joining Sigma Pi (it was not the fraternity which bears this name, but merely the literary society). There was a rival society known as Phi Alpha and I soon caught the college spirit and for six years was prepared to defend my society whenever it was challenged by the "Phis." From the start I took my part in the meetings, beginning with recitations and declamations and later in essays, orations, and debates. My work in the literary societies at Salem had given me some little experience, and yet before this new body of critics I found myself embarrassed by a feeling of timidity. My first appearance called forth more applause from my trembling knees than from the audience.

I may digress for a moment here to commend the work of literary societies. They are an important factor in school life, specially if one contemplates public speaking—an experience into which an increasing number are drawn when they are young though they may have no intention of entering public life.

Of the tasks that fall to the members of literary societies I put the greatest value upon declamations, essays, orations, and debates in the order named. The essay which is often read is, of course, easier to deliver than the declamation. The declamation, on the other hand, employs the words of another and does not require as much thought as the essay. The essay is the preparatory to the oration. It compels an originality of thought which is not necessary in declamation. The oration has all the virtues of the essay and adds to those the virtues of the declamation. It carries the student a step further. The debate is the climax of good speaking.

59

WILLIAM JENNINGS BRYAN

A debate brings out the ability of the essayist to think and to express himself with clearness and force. It also tests his ability to think upon his feet and to express himself without the aid of manuscript. But still more, it compels him to think quickly and to construct his replies on the moment. He analyzes his opponent's speech as it is made, takes its principal points and frames a reply without time for examination of authorities or for deliberation. The debate is superior also because it is the form of public speaking that wins the largest victories and gives the greatest renown. It gives the most conclusive proof of completeness of preparation, of a thorough understanding of the subject, of earnestness in its preparation, and therefore is most effective in its impression upon an audience.

CHAPTER III

AT THE BAR

POLITICAL opponents have sometimes referred to me as an unsuccessful lawyer; one president of a great eastern university in a campaign speech delivered in my home city in 1896 argued that I was unfit for the Presidency because I had never enjoyed a large income from my profession. I will not attempt to urge in my behalf the argument that turned Disraeli from the law to politics, that is: "To succeed as an advocate, I must be a great lawyer, and to be a great lawyer, I must give up my chance of being a great man"; but I think I owe it to my friends to give them a glimpse of my career as a lawyer. From this they can form an estimate as to whether I would have succeeded had I continued in the profession.

After graduating from the law school and after admission to the bar I returned to my home at Salem to prepare for a change in residence to Jacksonville, Illinois. During the preceding vacation (1882) I made a trip to Kansas City, which I had considered as a possible location. I was impressed by the reports of the growth of the city and went upon a tour of investigation.

I was deeply impressed with the size and bustle of the city, but was disturbed by the fear that I might not have money enough to support me until I could become self-supporting. If I had known as much about law business then as I learned afterwards I would not have been so timid about starting in a city, but the more I pondered over the problem the more strongly I was inclined to start in Jacksonville, where I thought the beginning would be easier. I reasoned thus: I had spent six years as a student at Jacksonville, was acquainted with many of the literary and business people there. I had graduated as the valedictorian of my class and was also class orator. I do not know whether others were ever guilty of the same error, but I am satisfied that I overestimated the impression that my college successes had made on the general public. But, mistake or no mistake, I decided to hang out my shingle in the charming little city which had come to seem like home to me after six years of student life there. So I planned to take my departure from Salem. I have been rather inclined to observe anniversaries and so I chose the Fourth of July for the date of my entering into Jacksonville—it was an easy day to remember and it gave me an anniversary that was sure to be generally observed.

Here again good fortune attended me. The law firm of Brown, Kirby, and Russell, one of the most, if not the most prominent in the city, was made up of three splendid men. William Brown was one of the ablest lawyers I have ever personally known. He was not only a most delightful companion but his way of addressing a judge or jury came nearer being ideal than that of any other person I have known. I think he had more influence upon my style of speaking than any other person from whom I have taken lessons. The friendship that grew up between us continued until he died, and my admiration for the man grew until he became so heroic a figure that I would have offered him a place in my cabinet had I been elected President.

Judge Edward P. Kirby was an admirable partner for a lawyer like Brown. The latter was a trial lawyer without a superior and with few equals; the former was an office lawyer, a man acquainted with pleadings and precedents and authorities, a man whom everybody trusted. He was especially consulted in any matters of probate and settling of estates.

Robert D. Russell, the third member of the firm, was younger than either of the others and one of the most lovable men it has been my lot to know. He was what is often called "the rising young lawyer," ready, diligent, and the friend of all who needed friends. They were all closely identified with Illinois College and within the circle of Dr. Jones' friends and it was possibly for that reason that I received the welcome they accorded me. Some six months after entering the firm, Mr. Russell, who was a brother of the great actor, Sol Smith Russell, moved to Minneapolis, which led to the turning over of much of the collection business of the office to me.

I remember with what anxious expectations I nailed up my modest sign, "W. J. Bryan, Lawyer," on the doorpost and awaited the rush of clients. I use the word "awaited" advisedly, because waiting was the word. It was then that I experienced my first disappointment. The people whom I knew personally seemed to have very little law business or were supplied with legal representatives. The days passed wearily. There was a continuous tread upon the stairs leading up to the second floor where the firm's offices were, and I would turn to the door each time I heard a hand upon the knob, only to find that the visitor had turned into the office of Mr. Brown, Mr. Kirby, or Mr. Russell. They had clients enough and were busy all the time, but the chair that I had been careful to provide and place at my desk stared at me vacantly.

One of my earliest clients was John Sheehan. He had worked for Dr. Jones when I made my home there. He took care of the doctor's horse, looked after the furnace, mowed the lawn, etc. When I opened my office he was keeping a saloon on East State Street. Soon after I began the practice he called to renew acquaintance and to tell me that, while he had a cousin practicing law, he was going to bring me all the business that he could. The reason he gave was that I was friendly to him when I was a student. This was one of the earliest instances—they have been numerous since—where I saw the return of bread cast upon the waters. It did not cost me anything to be friendly to John when he worked for the doctor. I was amply rewarded by the friendliness that John showed in return, and my impression upon him made him one of my first clients.

He said he knew that I was not in sympathy with his business, but that he thought I might be willing to collect some small bills that men owed him for liquor they had bought. I told him that I did not drink myself nor advise drinking, but that I thought those who bought liquor ought to pay for it. I think the first bill he gave me was for $2.60 and a note from me to the debtor brought a prompt settlement. John was very much pleased when I went to the door of his saloon, called him out, and counted out his $2.60, less twenty per cent commission; but what pleased John still more was that the man from whom I made the collection returned and again became a customer. This gave John an argument that he was quick to employ, as I had reason to know he told his friends that Mr. Bryan could collect a bill without making the man mad.

I was not slow to learn the lesson that this taught. I made it a practice not to make men mad when I was collecting bills. If the man could not pay at the time, I asked him to fix a day when I should call again. If he was not ready at the second call, it never annoyed me; I fixed another time. And so I continued to call until the bill was paid, often a little at a time. This sometimes made clients of the men from whom I collected bills.

I recall that Dr. Jones put some accounts in my hands, one of them against a liveryman. After he had postponed payment until I had called half a dozen times he said, "I could pay this bill if you could collect some bills for me and apply the amount, less your commission, on Dr. Jones' bills." I said, "Certainly," and he turned over a batch of accounts. It was not long before I had collected enough to cover the bill that I held against him and had some others besides. One of the bills brought me one of the first of a series of cases that gave me a good deal of satisfaction. One of the liveryman's bills was against a policeman and he wanted a credit of $25, I think it was, which the liveryman had offered as a reward for the recovery of a stolen horse. It seems that the liveryman had missed a horse one night and, thinking it had been stolen, had offered a reward. The policeman found the horse not long afterward tied not far from the livery stable and claimed the reward. The horse was so near and was found so soon that the liveryman did not think the finding came within the spirit of the offer. I looked the matter up and found that there was a city ordinance making it unlawful for a policeman to receive a reward for work done in the line of duty. I brought suit and having prepared myself on this point I plead the ordinance and defended it on the ground of public policy and won the suit. This success did not come until after the Devlin suit later referred to, but was the outgrowth of early collections.

At the end of each month I counted up my receipts— not a difficult task. I remember that at the end of one month my total receipts amounted to $2.50, and, a little discouraged, I wrote to my sweetheart something of my start in the law. After I had finished the letter and reported the meager returns a man came in and wanted an acknowledgment, for I was a notary as well as a lawyer, and I added a postscript saying that I had taken in twenty-five cents more that month. She wrote back a cheering letter saying that I should not be discouraged and that I was simply passing through the narrows. I replied that that was true if it meant that I was in straitened circumstances.

The outlook was so much less promising than I had anticipated that I entered into correspondence with Henry Trumbull, the son of Judge Lyman Trumbull, the law-school classmate I have referred to, with a view to trying my fortune in Albuquerque, New Mexico, where he had located, his choice being influenced largely by his threatened consumption. Between the Fourth of July and the first of January, nearly six months, my total receipts amounted to a little over $67, or an average of $11 a month.

With the beginning of the new year business picked up. The collections turned over to me by Brown and Kirby gave me a start. Dr. Jones found me a few clients and John Sheehan, whose enthusiasm had been increased by my success in collecting bills for him, brought me a really substantial client, out of whose business I made $200—three times my income for the first six months.

This client was Richard Larkin, an Irishman who had a little grocery store, and who, as I learned afterwards, handled liquors on a small scale. I was made assignee of Mr. Larkin's business, which included the collection of a large number of store accounts. These accounts brought me into acquaintanceship with a large percentage of the Irish who traded in Jacksonville and I made friends of his patrons. I was a persistent collector and a very patient one. It never annoyed me to have to call again and again. I may add here that I formed the practice of keeping my collections separate.

When I would collect a little bill I would take out my commission, put the balance in an envelope and put the envelopes away in a vault so that I could always pay my client the amount due him at any time. This custom of keeping clients' accounts separate was adopted upon the advice of my father. When my father last visited me—the visit which ended by his death—I was treasurer of the college paper and he noticed that I had in my bureau drawer an envelope containing money that I collected from advertisers and subscribers. When he inquired about the money I explained to him that it belonged to the college members and that I kept it by itself. He took occasion to commend and to advise me to follow that rule in regard to all money that I collected from others, saying that if I kept their money separate from my own I would not be tempted to make a temporary use of it and would always have it ready for my clients.

While Sheehan brought me the Larkin business Dr. Jones went on my bond as assignee.

My first lawsuit grew out of Mr. Larkin's business. I had an account against Mr. and Mrs. Matt Devlin. The sum was not large—somewhere between $30 and $40, I think. They objected to some items which he was not willing to omit and I brought suit. Mr. and Mrs. Devlin employed as their counsel Jerry Donahue, one of my classmates at college. When we graduated from Illinois College he studied law at Ann Arbor and I at Chicago. We returned to Jacksonville about the same time and this was his first suit as well as mine. It may seem a trifling thing to report, but a suit for that amount was not trifling to either of us at that time. Mrs. Devlin was an important member of the family and took the leading part in resisting payment. I distinctly recall the expression of disgust upon her face when I concluded my argument in support of my client's claim. She settled back in her chair and said, "Thank God, he's done." When the jury returned the verdict in my favor for the full amount it was with great difficulty that I restrained myself from giving utterance to a similar expression.

As time went on larger matters were brought to me and my clients increased in number and in business importance.

My first calendar year, January, 1884–85, showed receipts of something over seven hundred dollars. The second year something over a thousand, the third about fifteen hundred. As I removed to Nebraska at the end of nine months, the fourth calendar year was not completed. The receipts for nine months were nearly fourteen hundred dollars, making sure that that year would have shown a reasonable increase over the preceding one. I give these facts to show the growth of my practice. The beginning was about as small as it could well be, but the gain was constant and my prospects were equal at least to those of any young lawyer in the city of like age and experience. I had the confidence of the profession and the community, as one instance will illustrate. I had my small bank business with the First National Bank, whose president, Felix Ferrell, had been my Sunday-school teacher when I was in college. One day Mr. Brown came from his office to ask me to become assignee in bankruptcy for one of his clients. I responded in the affirmative. He then asked me whether Mr. Ferrell would go on my bond for $40,000. I told him that I had never asked him to go on my bond and could not answer until I had consulted him. Mr. Brown was connected with another bank and I told him that if Mr. Ferrell went on my bond I would want to give the assignee's account to his bank. This he readily assented to as fair and proper. Then he telephoned Mr. Ferrell, who immediately came to the office. I hope I will be pardoned for saying that what followed was a compliment that I have never ceased to appreciate. Mr. Ferrell was not a man of many words; neither was Mr. Brown; and the conversation was brief and to the point. Mr. Brown: "We want Mr. Bryan to act as assignee in bankruptcy for ——. Will you go on his bond for $40,000?" Mr. Ferrell: "Yes." Mr. Brown: "Thanks." Mr. Bryan: "I am much obliged."

While I was practicing I had the usual experience of young lawyers in being called upon to speak on many different occasions. The lawyer has the advantage over all others in such matters. He is the natural spokesman of those of his school of thought and he is called upon more at banquets than those of other professions, because in the course of business he has to deal with a greater variety of subjects. Every form of question comes before the court and the lawyer is really attending school all his life. Some one has said that every speech represents the sum of the man's knowledge. Consciously or unconsciously, the speaker uses all that he has learned as background for each effort.

AT THE BAR

As I look back over my life I am increasingly impressed with the important part played by little circumstances. They really shaped events. While they seemed trivial at the time, yet in retrospect we can see how the absence of any one of them would have broken the chain of causation. My removal to Nebraska and the events following it furnish numerous illustrations.

To begin with, the one thing that singled Lincoln, Nebraska, out from other Western capitals and gave me a special interest in it was the fact that Adolphus Talbot lived there. We had been in law school together from the fall of 1881 to the spring of 1883. We were members of the class of '83, Union College of Law, Chicago, Illinois. We had been meeting twice a day at recitations for some weeks when the following incident occurred. A lady who was on a visit to the family with which I boarded inquired whether I knew Dolph Talbot. Upon my replying that I knew him as one of the members of the class she proceeded to tell me about a very charming young lady to whom he was engaged. Knowing enough about Talbot to know that he was a jovial good-natured fellow, I thought I would have some fun with him, so I sat down by him when the class was assembling and before the lesson began made up a story about as follows:

"Talbot, when I came up here last fall I felt rather lonesome and advertised for unknown correspondents. A number of young ladies answered me, but after a few exchanges of letters I dropped all but one. She made such a favorable impression upon me that we continued the correspondence until we made known our real names. As she lives at Abington, where you graduated, I thought you might be able to tell me something about her." I then gave him the name of his own sweetheart.

I need not add that he was surprised. My joke was working well. He replied with evident seriousness, "If she is the Miss —— whom I know, she is a very nice girl."

WILLIAM JENNINGS BRYAN

Having obtained the information that I pretended to seek, I tried to change the subject, but he would not change it, and kept returning to the theme, much to my enjoyment. I could see that he was not taking much interest in the lesson that morning and when it was over he followed me downstairs, still returning to the young lady at Abington. I did not have the heart to leave him in suspense all day, so as we separated at the corner of Dearborn and Washington Streets I told him that it was just a joke suggested by the fact that I had that morning met a lady who told me of his engagement to Miss ——. He chased me for a block down the street until I dodged into the Rapier Building, where Judge Trumbull's office was located.

At the afternoon recitation Talbot hunted me up with a broad smile on his face and admitted to me that my joke had him "going," as they say. At the conclusion of the recitation we went out together and during our conversation I learned that we were practically of the same age, had graduated on the same day, had become engaged about the same time. Our fiancées, as we compared notes, seemed to stand out as quite superior to all other young ladies of that age. This was a beginning of a friendship which has for forty years been one of the most delightful that I have known.

I speak elsewhere of the partnership which was an outgrowth of this meeting; I refer to it here as one of numerous factors which combined to take me from Illinois to Nebraska and, in so doing, laid the foundation of my political career.

Some years later, while a member of Congress, I made a speech in Baltimore in which I referred in a humorous way to this incident and after tracing its influence up to the time that I was elected to Congress, concluded: "My election to Congress, therefore, may be regarded as a result of a joke which I played in college."

The man who followed me (I think it was Dr. Gonzales) convulsed the House by referring to my statement and adding, "To come to Congress as a result of a joke is not new; I have known men to go to Congress as a result of a joke they have played upon the whole community."

But to continue the chain of circumstances. In the spring of 1887 I still had desk room in the office of Brown and Kirby. A part of the work turned over to me by Brown and Kirby was the collection of interest on notes held by Illinois College as its endowment fund. Judge Kirby, who was treasurer of the Board of Trustees, suggested that I make a trip to Kansas to call personally on some of the makers of these notes. He explained to me that the college could not afford to do more than pay traveling expenses and a small commission on collections made. As I had never been West, the proposition appealed to me and I made plans for the trip.

When I spoke of the matter at home, my wife's father asked me whether it would be much out of my way to go to Creston, Iowa, and look at a tract of land there which he had held for many years. I examined the map and found that it was not far out of my way and decided to include Creston in the trip. Upon closer examination, I found that I could go from Kansas to Creston either by way of St. Joseph or via Lincoln. The fact that Talbot lived at Lincoln decided me to go by that route.

I reached Lincoln early on Saturday morning in July of 1887, was accorded a hearty welcome and spent that day and the Sunday following with my old law-school classmate. The joke, plus the errand upon which the college sent me, plus the fact that my father-in-law had a piece of land in Creston—the three combined to make me acquainted with Lincoln and the opportunities which it offered to a young lawyer. Here were three little circumstances, each one a necessary factor in my change of residence.

But even these would not have led to my removal to Lincoln had it not been for two other small circumstances. Just before I made the trip to Kansas I had decided to open up an office for myself and I had rented rooms next to Brown and Kirby's office—I had even gone so far as to re-paper the rooms and put them in order for my return from the West. But when I came back from Lincoln I was so deeply impressed with the advantages of the proposed change of location that I arranged for a transfer of lease and began to put my affairs in shape to leave for Nebraska in the autumn.

About the time I had rented the room and began planning for a separate office, I came near entering a partnership at Jacksonville which, if it had been formed, would have prevented my going to Nebraska and by so doing prevented the experiences which followed the change of residence. As I look back upon the little difference which prevented the formation of this partnership I am amazed at the influence that it had upon my life.

Richard Yates, son of Illinois' "war governor," who had graduated from Illinois College two years before my graduation, was the city attorney and a candidate for reëlection. We compared our incomes and found that his, including the city attorney's salary, was about the same as mine without any salary, and that therefore we could divide equally without material loss to either. But his salary constituted a considerable part of his income and he felt that it would not be fair for us to divide equally unless he should be reëlected. As the election was some considerable way off, I did not like to delay action in the matter of partnership until then and I proposed to him that I would take the nomination on the Democratic ticket so as to make sure that the salary would come into our office. To this he objected on the ground that his majority against me (I conceded that the chances were greatly in his favor) would not be as great as the majority he hoped to get against the Democrat who seemed likely to be nominated. Looking to a political life, he counted on the size of his majority to aid him in future candidacies.

AT THE BAR

As I recall this incident nearly thirty-five years ago, it seems to me that the two objections to the partnership were both trivial, my unwillingness to risk the small chance of his being defeated and his unwillingness to risk the small loss of majority that he might suffer from my candidacy; and yet these trivial objections prevented the formation of a partnership which would have kept me in Jacksonville.

Another circumstance quite as insignificant might have kept me in Illinois. After the election of President Cleveland in 1884, Mr. James Van Horbeck was appointed United States District Attorney at Springfield. He resided at Carlyle, Illinois, county seat of Clinton County, which was included in my father's judicial circuit when he was on the bench. Mr. Van Horbeck had practiced law under my father and had, I think, been admitted to the bar by him. For that reason he was personally friendly to me.

In the spring of 1887 I went to Springfield and consulted him about appointment as Assistant United States Attorney. He told me that he was not now ready to make the change, but that he would gladly give me the place when there was a vacancy but for the fact that he had promised it to a man endorsed by Congressman Springer. I returned to Jacksonville regretting that circumstances denied me the appointment.

The following September, while I was breaking up housekeeping preparatory for our departure for Nebraska, a carriage drove up to the door and the Assistant United States Attorney called to tell me that he was ready to resign and that the man to whom Mr. Van Horbeck had promised the Assistant's place had moved to Oklahoma and that I could have the position. But it was then too late. My plans had been completed and could not at that time be changed. I was sorry that the information had not come sooner, but if the appointment had been offered me before I went West I would have taken the position at Springfield and would not have gone to Nebraska.

WILLIAM JENNINGS BRYAN

Having laid before the reader the five little circumstances that had a part in my moving to Nebraska, I will only add here that I reached my new home just in time. If I had gone earlier I might have been involved in the divisions in the party and been less available at the particular time which was most favorable for my entrance into politics.

I have described how circumstances combined to take me to Lincoln, Nebraska, where I caught a vision that led to a change in residence. When I returned to Jacksonville I laid the matter before my wife, giving her the reasons for the change as they had impressed me.

First; While I was prospering in Jacksonville, it was only a question of a few years before I would reach the limit of possibilities and Lincoln was a city about four times as large as Jacksonville. Then, too, Lincoln was the capital of a state and I might expect Supreme Court business from outside counties. Illinois had passed through its period of rapid development; Nebraska was growing rapidly. I had found in Lincoln the owner of a weekly newspaper who offered to give me a column of his paper for the answer of legal questions submitted by his readers. This, I thought, would enable me to make acquaintances and become known to the people of the county. And then I had further found there my law-school friend Talbot, who offered me a partnership.

Every argument that impressed me was professional, no thought of politics ever entered my mind. How could it when Nebraska was a Republican state? The Congressional District to which I was moving was Republican; so was the county of Lancaster, the city of Lincoln, and the ward in which I expected to live.

When I had finished my argument my young wife answered in the spirit which she has always shown, "You know Jacksonville; you have seen Lincoln. If you think that the change is for the best, I am willing to go."

We had both attended school in Jacksonville and were

attached to a delightful circle of friends. It was hard to leave these and go to a new country. She was loath to leave the friends who had become so dear to us, and my regret was as deep as hers, but she left the decision to me.

Having obtained my wife's consent, I laid the matter before her father and I cannot forget the generous manner in which he met the situation. I presented to him the same arguments I had laid before my wife and told him of her answer and of my opinion. He replied, "Well, William, it does not make much difference to Lovina (his wife) and me where we live. It does make a difference to you and Mary. You do what you think is best for you and for her, and her mother and I will suit ourselves to your plans."

As a result of an impression more than as a result of clearly defined reasons the die was cast in favor of a change of residence. As I look back to that day I confess that I am somewhat bewildered. Not a single reason that led me to favor the change materialized, but reasons that I never saw and could not therefore take into account justified the change. As I shall show later, my professional success, while as great as we could reasonably expect, covered so brief a period that I could not test the opportunities which appeared to me large enough to justify beginning to practice law in a new state.

And so I arranged to leave for Nebraska on the last day of September and reached Lincoln on the first day of October, 1887, the third anniversary of our marriage. As it was too late in the fall to begin the construction of the home in Lincoln, it was decided that Mrs. Bryan would remain in Jacksonville during the winter with our child and my wife's parents and would join me when the house was completed. When we sold the Jacksonville home I found that Dr. Jones had never put on record the mortgage which I gave him when the house was built, an expression of confidence which I appreciated. The Nebraska home was built by my father-

75

in-law, Mr. Baird, and I rented it until I was in a position to buy it sometime later.

October first, 1887, was a beautiful autumn day. Talbot was at the station to welcome me and he there introduced me to two Democrats who were the beginning of my political friends in that state. One was R. P. Millar, the station agent of the Missouri Pacific Railroad in Lincoln, and W. B. Morrison, a resident of Hickman, about twenty miles south of Lincoln. The partnership of Talbot and Bryan began at once and our offices were in the First National Bank Building. Talbot was the local attorney for the Missouri Pacific Railroad, but it was understood that his salary and fees from the railroad were individual and not covered by the partnership. All other business was the firm's. It was not large at first, because Talbot's connection with the Missouri Pacific had taken him away from the office for a considerable portion of his time and his practice had suffered for lack of a partner.

My first fee came from a man by the name of O'Mara, an Irishman who had heard my Buckhorn School House speech. Although the fee was small, it was a pleasant reminder of the speech into which I had, for professional reasons, tried to inject a reference to my being a lawyer.

When I went to Nebraska I carried with me about $300, a fee which I had just earned in a lawsuit won in the Appelate Court. I also carried with me to Lincoln a letter of introduction to the German National Bank. Joseph Boehmer, the cashier of that bank, had come from Quincy to Lincoln and the letter was from Erwin Wood, who had known him in the former city. I deposited the $300 in the German National Bank and soon became its attorney. The business I received from the bank and through its influence aided me materially in the beginning. Soon after I located in Nebraska we moved our offices to the Burr Block, a building just completed at that time. As I was alone and as I wished to make my $300 go as far as possible, I saved room rent by sleeping on a folding lounge in the office. I economized on food also by buying twenty-one meal tickets for $4.50 at O'Dell's Restaurant and using them two a day instead of three. I ate in the morning and in the evening and contented myself with a lunch at noon, usually an apple and a few gingersnaps. I can remember with great distinctness when the office receipts became sufficient to justify the use of three meal tickets a day.

When I began practice anew in Nebraska my first work was in the matter of collections. I recall one small collection which fell into my hands soon after I joined Talbot. A client who had a little grocery store in the suburbs brought in a small bill which was owed him and told me that he thought the man would pay it if I wrote him a note to stir him up.

I wrote the usual note, framing it in language as polite as I could command, and awaited the call of the debtor. He never came, but the client dropped in the office a few days later to report. As he came into the outer room I noticed a smile upon his face which I interpreted to mean that my note had been successful. When he reached the door I greeted him with,

"Well, I sent him the note. Did it stir him up?"

"Stir him up?" he replied. "I should think it did." Then he took off his hat and showed me a lump nearly as large as an egg on the side of his head, explaining that the debtor had responded to the note, but had called upon him instead of upon his attorney and had hit him on the head with a brick!

I have often thought of this incident when in a campaign I would hear some one boast that he had stirred up the enemy.

I was always interested in the establishment of important legal principles, as two illustrations will show. Not long after I located at Lincoln, Editor Emmons of our local weekly Democratic paper, called on me for advice in regard to a lawsuit. He had been circulating cards advertising his newspaper among the delegates who had come in to attend the county convention. Some of them threw the cards upon the sidewalk and a policeman attempted to arrest Emmons for violating a city ordinance which forbade the throwing of paper upon the street. Emmons resisted arrest and came out second best in the encounter. He went to the office of a justice of the peace and filed complaint against the policeman for assault and battery and the constable refused to serve the papers without fees being advanced. Emmons wanted to know whether it was necessary for him to advance the fees in order to secure redress. I looked for authorities and could find none. One statute specifically gave the constable the right to demand fees before serving papers. After careful consideration of the facts I reached the conclusion in which Judge Cassidy, who was associated with me, concurred: that while the statute made no exception of papers served in criminal cases, such an exception must be presumed, otherwise redress for criminal assault would be impossible to those without means.

Pleading the case upon what I regarded as a fundamental principle, namely, that justice could not be sold and that a remedy in a criminal case could not depend upon the financial ability of the party injured, I drew a petition for a writ of mandamus compelling the constable to serve the warrant without prepayment of his fee. When I took the petition to Judge Chapman and told him the nature of my petition he shook his head and replied:

"You will have to have a very strong case before I will make an officer serve papers without fees being advanced."

"I have a strong case," I answered, "as I think I shall be able to convince you." At the hearing I did convince him and he issued the writ, from which the defendant appealed.

AT THE BAR

When the matter came up in the Supreme Court the hearing was held in a room on the walls of which appeared the seal of the state with the state's motto, "Equality before the law." As that was the basis upon which our fight was being made, I was able to point the judges to the state's motto and it doubtless had its effect in securing a decision, the first, I think, in the United States establishing this important principle. Neither Judge Cassidy nor myself received any fee in this case, but Emmons, who afterwards moved to Oklahoma, had a little post office in his county named after me.

Another case in which I took a deep interest brought me more satisfaction than money. Some beet-sugar factories were established in Nebraska soon after I went there and those in charge of the factories secured a state statute granting a bounty and also sought bounties of counties and precincts. One day a lawyer called with a letter of introduction from J. Sterling Morton to consult me about the legality of a bond issue voted in a precinct in which he lived. My recollection is that his vote was the only vote in the precinct against the bounty. But he wanted to oppose it on the ground that it was unconstitutional. He found me sympathetic. He paid me $25 down and was to pay $25 later. But the account remains open. The fee, however, was immaterial; the case gave me an opportunity to contest the constitutionality of a bounty and I was glad of the opportunity.

We decided to contest the issue of the bonds voted when an attempt was made to issue them. Before they reached this particular precinct a suit was brought to test the validity of similar bonds issued by an adjoining precinct. It was a friendly suit brought by the interested parties against the State Auditor to compel the registering of the bonds, both parties being for an affirmative order. I appeared at the trial and asked for permission to file a brief, stating to the court that I represented a client who was contesting bonds of the same kind in an adjoining precinct. Both sides objected to my request, but the court overruled the objections and allowed the brief to be filed.

When the court decided against the bonds, and in so doing disappointed both plaintiff and defendant, I had satisfaction enough to more than make up for the unpaid portion of my promised fee and was rewarded still further when as a member of Congress this experience enabled me to answer a question which was put to me by an Iowa Republican who knew of the bonds voted but did not know of the court decision nullifying them.

My first case in the Supreme Court came from Greeley County and involved a county-seat election. Those who have ever lived in a county where such elections take place need not be told that the interest in a presidential election is, in comparison, quite negligible. The question to be decided was whether the county seat should be removed from Scotia, a Union Pacific Railroad town on the edge of the county, to Greeley Center, a Burlington Railroad town near the center of the county. The railroads as well as the localities were interested and every voter in the county was at the polls, plus others.

General Barry and John Cavanaugh, two members of the election board, favored Greeley Center, where they lived, but as honest and conscientious officers they were compelled to throw out the vote of one precinct as fraudulent. After the vote was counted it gave the majority to Greeley Center, but Barry and Cavanaugh, true to their oath of office, acted against their personal interests and rejected this precinct.

When the case came up in the Supreme Court Scotia had her attorneys and Greeley Center had hers. The Scotia attorneys wanted the vote in question thrown out. Greeley Center wanted it counted in. Barry and Cavanaugh retained me to represent them as officials, explaining to me that, officially, they wanted me to defend their action, but they personally would like to have their action overruled.

It made my position a delicate one. There was no doubt in my mind about the fraudulent character of the disputed returns. I question whether any records present a case where the fraud was more transparent. The law required that the name of the voter be entered, and those who committed the fraud evidently had to act in a hurry; not having time to manufacture a list of names which would at least look honest, they put down prominent names of presidents, well-known senators, and distinguished men of other states.

In the trial I, of course, was on the side of Scotia and therefore acted with the Scotia attorneys. Before taking up the case on its merits, Scotia's attorneys moved for a delay, and at the request of my clients I joined with the Greeley Center people to oppose delay. This confused the court and one of the judges asked, "Mr. Bryan, for which side do you appear?"

I replied, "I had hoped that my argument would indicate that."

The judge said, "Your argument is clear enough, but I thought you were on the side of Scotia."

"I am," I said, "on the merits of the case, but I am with the attorneys of Greeley Center in opposing the motion." My clients had the pleasure of winning their case and the sorrow of seeing their city fail in its effort to secure the county seat.

Measured by its outcome, my removal to Nebraska was the gift of good fortune. I was most lucky in the selection of a law partner. Adolphus R. Talbot is a rare man—one of God's noblemen. In law school we had come to address each other as Dolph and Will and so when we united our energies in the practice of law, it was a very friendly union. We were about the same height and age, he nearly a year the older—from April around to March—about the same size and not far from the same weight. We were as much alike as two men could be and yet we were quite dissimilar in several respects. He was of English stock, having been born in England; I was very much mixed, with the Irish predominating in my name. He was a Methodist and I a Presbyterian; he was a Republican and I a Democrat. When baldness attacked us, his hair retreated from the front and mine from the rear. In the practice he looked at our side of the case and I inquired as to the arguments that the opposition could advance. But in spite of our points of dissimilarity, no two lawyers ever worked together with less friction. On the first of each month one would take his day book into the room of the other—whichever one happened to think of it first—and we would go over the credits and debits together, each would strike his balance and whichever had the largest net receipts would give the other a check for half and then we wrote "settled" across the two books and never had any other reckoning.

I mentioned the fact that he was a Republican and I a Democrat. At one time he was chairman of the Republican City Committee and I was chairman of the Democratic City Committee.

Our offices consisted of three rooms, the reception room and two private offices. When a man came in and inquired for the chairman of the Committee the clerk would ask him "of which committee?" He was still chairman when I ran for Congress and reported an incident that occurred during the campaign.

One of the members of the city committee called on him to say that he felt that he ought to resign as a member of the committee because he was going to support Bryan for Congress. Talbot assured him that that was not necessary, that the Republican candidate for Congress was only one of many candidates on that ticket and this was only one campaign. The man was finally persuaded not to give up his committeeship and I learned later that the chairman and more than half the committee were supporting me. During my campaign of 1896 Mr. Talbot was a Republican candidate for the Nebraska State Senate and was embarrassed by seeing published in the Lincoln papers glowing eulogies of me which he had written to papers in other states in answer to inquiries.

Talbot's personal friendship was always greater than his Republicanism, despite his prominence in the party. For more than thirty years he has been one of my nearest and dearest friends. Whenever I am relieved for a moment from the pressure under which I have lived, a pressure so great as to prevent any leisurely review of the past or unhurried contemplation of the future, and I allow myself to think of the latter days, I dream of a brief period before the close of life when, my work done, I can commune with lifelong friends and recall the joint struggles of early days. I always think of Dolph as one of those with whom companionship will be most satisfying.

When I was elected to Congress, I felt that I should give my entire time to my work and therefore I turned over to Mr. Talbot the unfinished business and only appeared where it was necessary to please some particular friends among our clients. The only conflict of opinion we ever had over fees was when I went to Congress. He insisted on giving me a larger percentage of the fees which came from the left-over business than I thought I deserved and it was not without a good deal of argument that we reached a compromise of our differences.

The firm name was continued while I was in Congress and I expected to resume the practice when I returned to Lincoln in 1895, but by that time the fight over bimetallism was just beginning and I received about the same time three invitations from widely different points, one to answer John Sherman at Salem, Oregon, another to answer him at Cincinnati, Ohio, and a third to answer John G. Carlisle at Memphis, Tennessee. It soon became apparent that I must either refuse political invitations or suspend practice again. I was too much interested in the fight for which I had helped to lay the plans to disappoint those whom I had helped to enlist, and so I decided to postpone for another year my return to law.

Then came the Presidential campaign of 1896 which so completely identified me with national politics that I felt that I must keep up the fight for at least another four years. So I retired from the firm.

My last appearance as a member of the Nebraska bar was in the United States Supreme Court in a maximum rate case which arose over a law passed in Nebraska and contested by the railroads. The Attorney-General of Nebraska, Hon. C. J. Smythe, one of my closet political friends, represented the state. I was so deeply interested in the result of the trial that I volunteered to appear without pay in order to present the one point in which I was concerned.

The proposition upon which I based my argument was taken from a book written by Governor Larrabee of Iowa, who became a leader of the agriculturists of that state in their effort to secure reasonable railroad rates. I read the book soon after I entered Congress and attempted to secure the incorporation of the principle in a pooling bill that passed the House while I was a member. My amendment to that bill was defeated, but it attracted enough attention to call forth one of the earliest epithets applied to me. A Richmond, Virginia, paper quite conspicuous for its sympathetic support of the corporation side of public questions, had an editorial denunciation of my amendment which appeared under the title of "Nihilist Bryan."

CHAPTER IV

The Lure of the College Prize

I FELT the lure of prizes from the start and took part in every contest for which I was eligible. A prize always stirred me to activity, and a recollection of its influence upon my studies has led me in later days to stimulate students to similar activity by the establishing of prizes in a number of institutions of learning.

The principal prizes I established were in the public school at Normal, the precinct in which our country home near Lincoln was located, and in some nineteen institutions —seventeen of them state universities—in which I established a prize for the best essay on the science of government. When, some years later, Mr. Philo S. Bennett consulted me in regard to the best use of some money which he desired to leave by will, I recommended similar prizes and upon his death distributed for him funds for the establishment of such prizes in twenty state universities.

In my first year in the academy—"Junior Prep" as it was called—I entered the declamation contest, using as my theme Patrick Henry's famous speech, "Give me liberty or give me death." The judges did not seem to regard me as especially promising. At any rate, I was not near enough to even second place to give me any intense interest in the returns. The next year I entered the declamation contest again, this time taking as my subject by the advice of Mrs. Jones, "The Palmetto and the Pine." The sentiment was most excellent, but my delivery seemed to lack something— enough to enable two of the contestants to pass me. I came third in the estimate of the judges and Dr. Jones thought that my failure may have been due to indistinctness of articulation. I do not know whether that was true or not, but it spurred me up on that particular subject and distinctness of articulation became a controlling passion with me.

In the freshman year I entered the declamation contest for the third time, after having divided the second prize in Latin prose composition with a fellow student. I was gaining ground. In my first contest I came down toward the last, in my second contest I ranked third, in my third contest I won half of the second prize, in my fourth contest— freshman declamation—I rose a point higher and had the second prize all to myself. I did not like dramatic pieces, but at the earnest solicitation of my instructor in rhetoric I took Bernardo del Carpio for my freshman declamation. Of course, the matter was very much on my mind during the days immediately preceding the contest, so much so that a night or two before the declaimers were to appear in public on the stage of Strawn's Opera House I had a dream that made an indelible impression upon me because it came true. In my dream, we seemed to have finished our declamations and were awaiting the announcement of the award of the prizes—a moment of great suspense, as all will admit who have passed through the experience. Then the chairman of the committee of judges appeared and wrote upon the blackboard the names of the victors. I could see my name very distinctly occupying the second place, but I could not make out the name of the man who was awarded the first prize.

My dream not only assured me of my success in securing second prize but it even disclosed to me the books which I selected (the prizes were given in books to be selected by the students themselves. The second prize in this case was $10.00). I selected an Oxford Bible with a concordance and a volume of Shakespeare. As I am writing these words I turn to this treasure and find on the first page of the Bible the following: at the top the Greek letters Sigma Pi and my class '81 and following that these words: "Presented to W. J. Bryan, Salem, Illinois, by the faculty of Illinois

THE LURE OF THE COLLEGE PRIZE

College, May 28, 1878. Second prize in declamation."
The copy of Shakespeare bound in calf is still in my library
and on the first page is a duplicate of the first page of the
Bible above referred to.

I digress here to say that I received the usual training in
public speaking. Professor Hamilton was our instructor;
he was a large man with a strong face and a piercing eye.
He rather leaned to the dramatic and recommended dramatic pieces to us. I rather preferred the oratorical style.
He complimented me by saying that I declaimed the oratorical pieces so well that he could not be of much assistance to
me along that line. He trained us in modulation of the
voice, gesticulation, etc., and I presume that his instructions
were beneficial to me, although I have been so much more
interested in the subject matter than in the form of presentation that my use of his advice has been unconscious
rather than intentional.

As our absorption of ideals is gradual and constant, I
do not know to what extent I am indebted to him for the
settled opinions which I have formed on public speaking. I
think that instruction in gesticulation becomes valuable as
one forgets the instructions and moves his arms and body
without thought of the instructions. It is hard to be
graceful in gesticulation when one is thinking about the
movements to be made, just as it is difficult for one to speak
naturally while he is engaged in artificial effort. But the
training that one receives, both in the modulation of the
voice and in action, finally becomes a part of him—a second
nature, so to speak—and he obeys the suggestions that he
has received without a thought.

In my sophomore year I entered the contest in essay and
won the first prize—my first first prize—with an essay on
the by no means novel subject of "Labor." This pleased
my father more than the previous prizes won. He said that
he would rather have me gain prominence for my own thought
than by repeating the words of others.

WILLIAM JENNINGS BRYAN

In my junior year I entered the oratorical contest influenced by a double ambition, because the successful orator in this contest would, as a matter of custom, represent the college in the intercollegiate contest the following fall. My subject on this occasion was "Individual Power" and I left nothing undone that would contribute towards success. I had had in mind for nearly five years the honor of representing the college in the oratorical contest. It so happened that soon after my arrival in Jacksonville I had the privilege of attending a contest in which Fred Turner, the orator of Illinois College, represented our institution. From that night this vision was before me and my work as a declaimer, as an essayist, and in the delivering of orations was to this end. I was successful—securing the first honor here as in the contest in essay the year before.

Possibly another digression here may be excusable. My good wife often refers to it when someone has in later years commented as to what they have described as the ease with which I speak. She says that they do not know how hard and for how many years I worked as a college boy and as a young man when I was in training. The incident which she often related is as follows. The contest came in May, 1880, some seven months after we became acquainted. Mrs. Jones, who was very fond of Miss Baird, conceived the idea of having a May Day party out in a woods pasture belonging to Dr. Jones. It so happened that this woods pasture adjoined the grounds of an insane asylum and it also happened that a man who had formerly worked for Dr. Jones was cultivating a farm close by this spot selected for the party. I went out to the grove an hour or so ahead of the rest of the party and spent the time delivering my oration with the trees as an audience. When Miss Baird and the other members of the May Day party approached the woods pasture the former employee left his plow and ran out to the road waving his hand in warning, calling out: "Don't go in there. There is a man over there shouting and waving his hands. I think he must have escaped from the asylum." Mrs. Jones and my wife-to-be guessed at once the cause of his alarm and entered the pasture in a mood to enjoy the day.

In the following October (1880) I went to Galesburg, Illinois, to represent my college in the contest to which I had looked forward for many years. My subject was "Justice." After the prize had been awarded, General John C. Black of Chicago, with whom I afterwards served in Congress, one of the judges in this contest, took me to his room in the hotel and gave me encouragement and advice. He told me that he had marked me one hundred on delivery and high enough on thought and composition to make me his first choice (the marks of the other two brought me down to second place). He then gave me his advice on various styles of oratory, contrasting the style of Edmund Burke, whose sentences were long and involved, and the style of Victor Hugo, whose sentences were short and pithy. He said that I leaned rather to the style of the latter and advised me to cultivate longer sentences. I have not forgotten his advice, but have found it difficult to follow it, possibly because I have always labored under the coercion that made me so anxious to present a subject clearly that I could not give much attention to ornamentation and figures of speech.

In my oration on "Justice" my introduction was, I think, as appropriate as any that I have ever employed. I learned quite early the wisdom of a beginning that immediately catches the attention. I noticed this in speeches, of which I early became an eager reader, and observed in Wendell Phillips when he delivered his famous lecture, "The Lost Arts," at Jacksonville during my student days. The great orator was in the habit of commencing with some reference to some local object of interest, which he linked to his address. Dr. Conwell employs the same art in his remarkable lecture on "Acres of Diamonds."

As it is my purpose to make my memoirs as useful as possible to the young people who read them, I am led to add that Paul has given to the public speakers of the world probably the most perfect illustration of easy and felicitous entrance on the presentation of a theme. His speech at Athens was before the most critical of his audiences and he was especially happy in selecting an opening phrase which at once enlisted the attention of his hearers:

"Ye men of Athens, I perceive that in all things ye are too superstitious.

"For as I passed by, and beheld your devotions, I found an altar with this inscription, TO THE UNKNOWN GOD. Whom therefore ye ignorantly worship, him declare I unto you.

"God that made the world and all things therein, seeing that he is Lord of heaven and earth, dwelleth not in temples made with hands;

"Neither is worshipped with men's hands, as though he needed any thing, seeing he giveth to all life, and breath, and all things;

"And hath made of one blood all nations of men for to dwell on all the face of the earth, and hath determined the times before appointed, and the bounds of their habitation;

"That they should seek the Lord, if haply they might feel after him, and find him, though he be not far from every one of us:

"For in him we live, and move, and have our being; as certain also of your poets have said, For we are also his offspring.

"Forasmuch then as we are the offspring of God, we ought not to think that the Godhead is like unto gold, or silver, or stone, graven by art and man's device.

"And the times of this ignorance God winked at; but now commandeth all men every where to repent:

THE LURE OF THE COLLEGE PRIZE

"Because he hath appointed a day, in the which he will judge the world in righteousness by that man whom he hath ordained; whereof he hath given assurance unto all men, in that he hath raised him from the dead." (Acts 17: 22–31.)

My speech on Justice began: "Plutarch tells us that men entertain three sentiments concerning the gods; they fear them for their power, respect them for their intelligence, and love them for their justice." The local paper had a complimentary account of my speech—they generally praised where they could performance of students—and these early bits of eulogy are very satisfying to participants in contests—especially those who fail to win prizes. I came second, my college backer insisting, as college boys are wont to do, that I ought to have had first place.

The fifty dollars handed me by the treasurer of the oratorical association was the largest sum that I had earned up to that time. The first draft upon me was made for the purchase of an engagement ring for my intended wife. I had waited from June until October in order to purchase the ring with money that I had myself earned. It was a modest ring—a garnet set in gold—but it was sufficient to satisfy our simple tastes, and adorn Mrs. Bryan's hand until it was lost during the campaign of 1896. It was my custom to earn the money to pay for any gifts to Miss Baird, and during a large part of my college days I added to my spending money by clerking in a hat store on Saturdays.

This contest was quite an event in college life and, as was customary, a delegation of the students went along to boost for their representatives. I had gone upon a similar expedition when Richard Yates represented our college and won the first prize at Champaign, Illinois, two years before. The successful competitors in a number of these inter-collegiate contests contested for the interstate prize at a later meeting which was at the time held in Jacksonville. By winning second prize I became the alternate and would have represented the state at the interstate contest had the winner of first prize failed to appear. Although this was a very remote contingency, I prepared myself for it, but Mr. Erskine, orator of the state at Galesburg, was there and I not only had no opportunity to enter the larger contest but was the victim of a good deal of ridicule when the man who defeated me came near the close of the list in the interstate contest. For several days I was greeted by college friends with substantially the same question: "If Erskine came last, where would you have been?"

At the Galesburg meeting, I was, because of my residence at Jacksonville, the place of the next contest, made vice-president of the interstate association. The work of arrangement fell to President Montgomery of Indiana and Secretary Howard of Iowa. In the correspondence that took place prior to the date of the contest at Jacksonville I was in correspondence with Montgomery and Howard. We had never met, but in the intimacy between us developed by the correspondence we had exchanged guesses as to each other. Howard and I discussed Montgomery, Montgomery and I discussed Howard, and Howard and Montgomery discussed me. When the time came for the meeting Montgomery and Howard arrived at Jacksonville at the same time and our acquaintance ripened into a permanent friendship. Judge Montgomery has since held a high judicial position in his state and I have frequently enjoyed the hospitality of his delightful home when I visited Seymour, Indiana. Howard afterward moved to Indianapolis and then to New York and was a Republican in his early days. He became a supporter of mine in 1896 and until his death in New York some years ago was a colaborer in the political vineyard.

I was a contestant for one prize in my senior year and there I came second, but I was even more pleased to have the prize go to Sam Eveland than to have won it myself. Sam was one of the lovable members of the class and one of the most interesting men I ever knew. He was brought up in Michigan. His education was neglected and he went early into the logging camps. As a young man he tramped from section to section in search of work. He went by chance one evening into a church where a protracted meeting was in session. He was converted and decided to be a minister. With Sam it was really a new birth. His life was as completely changed as was the life of Paul. I have never known a man more completely consecrated to the service of God and to the life patterned after the example of Christ.

He went to school in spite of the embarrassment that a grown person finds in studying with children. He was fourteen years older than myself, and I graduated at about twenty-one. I was about the average age for the class. He was not a brilliant man, but no one could surpass him in industry and in patient plodding. He was as truthful as a child; everybody loved him. When the professor of political economy announced "Pauperism, Its Causes and Remedies," as the subject of the thesis and that each member was expected to write, I remarked that we might each give our experience and let the prize go to the one who knew most about the subject, and that is the way it went. Sam Eveland won the prize. Evidence, if evidence was needed, of the value of personal knowledge in the presentation of any subject.

Still another digression here. When I went home to spend the Christmas holidays I went out to the county poorhouse, thinking that I might get some information for my thesis. I acquainted the superintendent with the object of my visit and he gave me access to the inmates. The first man I met was, to my surprise, a brother of one of the most prominent citizens of the county, a man of wealth, family, and influence. I found that this inmate was an unmarried man. My questions did not bring out much information beyond the fact that he had not saved anything and found himself a pauper during his later days. The second man whom I met was also unmarried and I jotted down "celibacy" as a cause of pauperism.

I began in my mind to sketch the path of the unmarried man without responsibility, he gives free rein to his desires and pleasures, wasting his life in enjoyment, and finally comes down to old age with no provision made for the days of failing strength. I thought I had made some progress in preparing my case. Then I met the third inmate.

"Are you married?" I enquired.

"Yes, my fourth wife left me when I came here."

"Have you any children?"

"Twenty-six." And my first theory was exploded.

After time for reflection I thought that possibly there might be a golden mean—that was before the word "golden" had been made odious by bad association—between the irresponsibility of the unmarried man and the burdened spouse and father. I have not yet been able to understand how a man could raise twenty-six children without having at least one among them who could care for him in his old age!

Returning to Eveland again: I cannot resist the temptation to record facts that come to my memory when the name of this dear friend is recalled. First was one of his experiences in courtship. I was rather a patriarch among the boys during my last year in college. I reached my twenty-first anniversary less than three months before graduation and I was engaged, as they say, during my entire senior year. This was known among the boys and some of them came to me for advice—among them Sam.

He took me aside one day and with evident emotion told me that he had at last found the girl for whom he was looking. He described her to me and according to his description she would make a model wife for a pastor. He

94

said that he had laid his claims before her the night before and that she had accepted him.

I was rather surprised at the suddenness with which he had proposed and suggested to him that it might have been better to have gone about it more gradually, but he was a very practical sort of a fellow and, having found the kind of wife for whom he was looking, he did not see why any period of romance should be injected between the discovery and the filing of his claim. I congratulated him, though I confess it was with some misgivings as to whether the agreement reached was really conclusive.

A few days afterward the poor fellow came to me distressed beyond description to tell me that he had called upon the young lady again and found that she did not understand that they were engaged. In fact, it was not long before he brought back that familiar report that while she could not marry him she would always be his friend. Later he was more successful and found an exemplary lady about his own age who was deeply religious and who became his wife.

The day before his marriage, he called on me. "Bryan," he said, "I want you to do me a favor. As I am a minister, I am afraid that the preacher who will officiate will not be willing to accept a fee from me. So I will give you the money and you can hand it to him."

Of course I responded favorably, and took the coin away with me in my pocket. Between that hour and the hour when he and his chosen one were to be united in the holy bonds of wedlock I framed a little speech to be made to the minister when it came time to act as Sam's paymaster. Everything went well. The invited guests were as happy as the bride and groom, the pastor was on hand and the ceremony was duly performed. After the congratulations I took the minister off to one side and began to deliver Sam's message. When I reached the proper point I put my hand into my pocket and to my amazement discovered that I had changed my trousers. The minister had to take my word for the fee until I could go home and get the money and hunt him up. Whenever I saw Sam afterward and we became reminiscent, this embarrassing episode was sure to be recalled. But my, what a smoke a little fire kindleth! All these recollections were unloosed when I thought of being defeated in a thesis contest by a classmate who had once been a tramp.

CHAPTER V

EARLY NATIONAL CONVENTIONS

I FORMED early the habit of attending national conventions. It so happened that the Democratic National Convention of 1876 was held in St. Louis, only seventy miles from my birthplace. My father and mother were attending the Philadelphia Exposition at the time, but my enthusiasm reached a point where I decided to go to the convention with some of the other boys—I do not recall that any of them were as young as myself. I sold enough corn to secure the small amount necessary, the railroad fare being only a few dollars and my other expenses being small. I recall that I stayed all night at East St. Louis, sleeping in a room with more than thirty others on cots.

Next day I appeared at the convention hall, but not knowing anyone from whom I could secure a ticket, I had to content myself with standing around watching the distinguished Democrats, to me unknown, go in and out of the convention. But here again my lucky star helped me out. A policeman, taking pity on me, put me in through a window and I had the pleasure of hearing John Kelly make his famous speech against Tilden. That was my initiation into national politics. Since that time I have attended every Democratic National Convention but three, and I was in close touch by wire with two of the three, those of 1900 and 1908. The Cincinnati Convention of 1880, therefore, is the only one that I have actually missed since I was sixteen years old. I was still a college boy in 1880 and Cincinnati was so far from Salem that I was able to withstand the temptation which overpowered me four years before.

When the convention of 1884 was held at Chicago I was living at Jacksonville, but my income was so meager that I decided that I could not afford a trip to Chicago, but here

again fortune favored me. I was invited to deliver a
Fourth of July address at Greenwood, not many miles from
Jacksonville. In accepting the invitation I answered the
inquiry about compensation by saying that I expected
nothing more than my traveling expenses. When I was
through speaking, the chairman of the committee asked me
about my expenses. When I stated the amount, something
less than three dollars, he handed me a twenty-dollar bill
with the remark,

"That will cover your expenses."

I was so surprised that I almost forgot to thank him.
I decided that I would construe my good luck as a providen-
tial provision for convention expenses and arranged to go
to Chicago. On the train I fell in with Carl Epler, son of
Judge Epler, one of the circuit judges presiding in the
Jacksonville circuit, and we made the trip together.

At Chicago we went from one headquarters to another
and listened to the arguments in favor of the various candidates. My personal preference was Senator Bayard of
Delaware. In one of the senates of which I was a member
when a schoolboy I represented Delaware and took the
name of Senator Bayard. I was open to conviction, however, and ready to hoorah for the candidate who won the
nomination.

As it is in all national conventions, it was difficult to get
a ticket of admission. Finding Hon. Telas W. Merritt, of
Salem, a prominent politician at the Illinois headquarters,
I asked him if he could secure tickets for Epler and myself.
He said he could not secure any tickets, but that he knew
one of the doorkeepers, whereupon he took us to Joseph
Chesterfield Mackin, a Chicago politician, and said in his
stammering way—he stuttered—"Joe, pa-pa-pass these
b-b-boys in." Joe passed us in and we returned to his door
regularly during the sessions of the convention. I am sorry
to have to remark in passing that Joe was soon after sent
to the penitentiary for "ballot-box stuffing"—this was

through no fault of Mr. Merritt's or of ours and I only mention it because I never think of the incident without also thinking of what befell Joseph Chesterfield after we had thus become acquainted with him.

When the 1888 convention was held in St. Louis I was a resident of Nebraska. Having helped elect Hon. J. Sterling Morton a delegate, I had no difficulty in getting a ticket to this convention. I remember being very much impressed by a nominating speech made by Senator Daniel of Virginia.

The Democratic National Convention of 1892 was held at Chicago. I was a member of Congress then and was renominated a few days before the convention, in fact, went from the Congressional Convention to the Chicago Convention. By this time I had become acquainted with a good many public men and also with a good many politicians. I spoke at Creston in the Boies Campaign the fall of 1891. Here I met a prominent Democratic politician of that section by the name of Duggan. I happened to meet him at Chicago and learned from him that he was doorkeeper. He offered to let any of my friends in and I soon found out how easily one could add to his list of friends when he could reward them with admission to the national convention. Before the sessions were over I had put a liberal number of western Democrats under obligation to me by bringing them into acquaintance with Mr. Duggan.

At the Chicago Convention I heard Bourke Cockran make his celebrated speech against the third nomination of Mr. Cleveland, but took no part in the convention's deliberations.

In 1896 I began attending Republican Conventions as well as those of my own party. The first was the McKinley Convention, which was held at St. Louis about two weeks before the Chicago Convention at which I was nominated. I was at that time editor of the *World-Herald* and attended the convention ostensibly in the character of a newspaper man. As a matter of fact, however, I was there to encourage the Silver Republicans in the fight they were making. Beginning in 1893, I had been more and more intimately acquainted with the Silver Republicans like Senators Teller, DuBois, Pettigrew, and Cannon, and Congressmen Shafroth, Towne, Hartmann, and others. I was in conference with them during the course of the fight over the platform and sent back editorial correspondence to my paper.

The convention turned out as I expected and the looked-for bolt took place. I felt sure that the action of this convention would have a large influence at Chicago.

CHAPTER VI

A Brief History of the Chicago Convention

FOR some months prior to the Chicago Convention of 1896, I had received letters from different parties in different states suggesting my candidacy. John W. Tomlinson, a delegate from Alabama, wrote me; Mr. Cassady, a delegate from Mississippi; Mr. Felix Regnier, a delegate from Monmouth, Ill.; Hon. M. A. Miller, a delegate from Oregon; Gov. J. E. Osborn, of Wyoming; Ex-Gov. Baxter, of Wyoming, and a number of others. They all presented the same arguments, and the arguments presented were the ones that led me to believe that there was a possibility of my nomination.

During the year 1895 I visited Springfield at the invitation of bimetallists and spoke at a convention which was the beginning of the organizing of the silver forces of that state. I met Governor Altgeld there and have letters which I received from him afterward suggesting the possibility of my receiving the nomination for Vice-President, he being favorable to Congressman Bland for President.

When I delivered my Tariff Speech in Congress in March, 1892, I received a telegram from a friend in Jacksonville which ran about as follows: "How old are you? Am for you for the Democratic Presidential Nomination if you are old enough."

This was one of the earliest outbursts of enthusiasm. From time to time newspapers mentioned my name in connection with the nomination. This occurred with increasing frequency after my Silver Speech in August, 1893. I had prepared the address on Bimetallism signed by some thirty-three members of Congress and had given it to the public about the fifth of March, 1895. I prepared it after consulting with Mr. Bland, whom we all recognized as the

101

leader of the silver forces in Congress. I had him sign it first, and I signed it second. No senators, as I recall it, signed it, and only about one fifth of the Democratic members. Others to whom it was presented objected on the ground that it might divide the party. A short time after that appeal was published, President Cleveland wrote a letter to a Chicago Club, in which he indicated that the fight was to be on the money question, and this aroused the silver Democrats to the realization of the fact that they would have to control the organization or be read out of the party. A conference was called for June at Memphis, Tenn. There the Democratic Bimetallic League was organized with Democratic senators as its officers. I attended this conference at Memphis—in fact, I had spoken in Memphis a month before in answer to Mr. Carlisle. He went to Memphis to deliver an address intended to line up the South in favor of the gold standard.

For the next year I traveled throughout the country, lecturing in some places and making public speeches in other places—everywhere helping, as best I could, in the organization of the silver forces. At Wilmington, Delaware, I paid the hall rent and introduced myself, and spoke to a handful of people in a small room. At one other place I helped to pay the expense of the meeting. It was through these speeches that I became acquainted with a number of the delegates who were present at Chicago. I perhaps was personally acquainted with more delegates than any other man who was mentioned as a candidate. My own state would have instructed for me if I had permitted it, but I objected on the ground that I did not want to be presented as a candidate for two reasons. First, there was no likelihood of my being instructed for in any other state, and, second because I wanted to help other men who were candidates to secure their own states.

I went to Chicago a few days before the Convention to

confer with the leaders who were making their plans for the control of the convention and was present when Senator Daniel was selected for temporary chairman. We already had a majority of the delegates instructed for bimetallism. At that time the sentiment seemed to be divided between Bland and Boies and Matthews, and as I looked over the situation, I did not think that the outlook for my candidacy was encouraging. In fact, I told Mr. Tomlinson that I did not want him to feel bound by his pledge to me if he found it to his advantage to support some one else. He gave me an insight into his political purpose when he told me that he had no interests of his own to advance, and that, as he still believed I was the most available candidate, he preferred to advocate my nomination whether there was any chance of my success or not.

I had an engagement to speak at the Chautauqua in Crete, Nebraska, between the preliminary conference at Chicago and the convening of the Convention. I was advertised for a debate there with John Irish of Iowa, one of the prominent advocates of the gold standard. I went to Nebraska to fill this engagement and then returned to Chicago with the Nebraska delegation. In the debate with Irish I used the sentence with which I closed my Chicago Speech—the sentence which refers to "the cross of gold and the crown of thorns." I had used it a few times before that time, recognizing its fitness for the conclusion of a climax, and had laid it away for a proper occasion.

Some of my friends spoke of me for temporary chairman of the Convention, but this position, as I have said, went to Senator Daniel, and a very wise selection it was. Then there was some talk of me for permanent chairman and this seemed a possibility when I made the brief trip to Nebraska. On the train I made some preparations in anticipation of an opportunity to speak at the Convention, although there was no certainty that this opportunity would come to me.

103

WILLIAM JENNINGS BRYAN

While I spent all my spare time in arranging the arguments for any speech that I might deliver at the Convention, I prepared only one new argument and that I have always regarded as the most important argument presented, although it has never received a great deal of attention from those who have commented upon the speech. I do not recall that it has ever received prominent attention until recently, when it was selected in England as the passage to be quoted in a description of that speech published in London. The passage reads as follows and was intended for a double purpose: first, to awaken small business men to an appreciation of their importance; and, second, to rebuke the gold advocates who were continually talking about business men but who regarded those engaged in big business as the only business men to be considered:

"We say to you that you have made the definition of a business man too limited in its application. The man who is employed for wages is as much a business man as his employer, the attorney in a country town is as much a business man as the corporation counsel in a great metropolis; the merchant at the crossroads store is as much a business man as the merchant of New York; the farmer who goes forth in the morning and toils all day—who begins in the spring and toils all summer—and who by the application of brain and muscle to the natural resources of the country creates wealth, is as much a business man as the man who goes upon the board of trade and bets upon the price of grain; the miners who go down a thousand feet into the earth, or climb two thousand feet upon the cliffs, and bring forth from their hiding places the precious metals to be poured into the channels of trade are as much business men as the few financial magnates who, in a back room, corner the money of the world. We come to speak for this broader class of business men."

104

HISTORY OF CHICAGO CONVENTION

When I got back to Chicago the situation, so far as my prospects were concerned, had not perceptibly improved and I found that my first fight would be to get my delegation seated, it having been shut out of the temporary organization by action of the National Committee in which the Gold Men had a considerable majority.

I might add here that the night before I made my speech in the Chicago Convention, the North Carolina delegation held a meeting, and as the majority of the delegation voted in favor of my nomination, the entire delegation was given to me by the unit rule, and I was so notified by one of the delegates, I think it was Mr. Josephus Daniels, who was national committeeman that year, and has so continued up to this day. Before the delivery of my speech I had assurances from several other states. I think that a majority of the Kansas delegation had indicated a preference for me in case Bland was not nominated. Senator Patterson has since told me of an incident that impressed him.

Senator Towne and Congressman Hartman were with Senator Patterson, and they came over to ask me to support Senator Teller. As Senator Patterson relates it, I listened to their arguments and when they were through, said to them that I did not regard Senator Teller's nomination as a possibility, that I was perfectly willing to vote for him myself because I regarded the money question as the paramount issue, but that we had won our fight in the Democratic party while the Republicans had lost their fight in the Republican party, and that it was easier to bring the disappointed Republicans over to the Democratic party than to carry the victorious Democrats over to the Republican party. Knowing that the gold Democrats would vote, I thought they could make a much stronger fight against one who, up to that time, had been identified with the Republican party, than against one who had been all his life a Democrat.

I still believe the reasoning sound, and I say this after reflection upon the ability, character, and patriotism of

Senator Teller, whom I then admired and for whom my admiration has grown with more intimate acquaintance. When I stated that I did not believe Senator Teller could be nominated, Senator Patterson asked me who could be nominated, and I told him that I thought I had as good a chance to be nominated as anyone, for by that time I thought I saw a considerable improvement in my chances. He asked me what strength I had in the Convention. I told him that Nebraska would be for me whenever I wanted its vote, that half of the Indian Territory would be for me on the second ballot, and I was intending to give the rest of my strength as far as I had learned it (I am not sure whether North Carolina had acted then or later in the evening); but before I could go any further, some one came up and interrupted the conversation, and Senator Patterson and his associates, not considering the matter of sufficient importance to wait longer, took their leave.

The Senator has told me with some amusement of the conversation that followed when he, Mr. Towne, and Mr. Hartman reached the street. They looked at each other and smiled at the presumption of a man who calculated on the presidential nomination with only his own state back of him and the Indian Territory on the second ballot. Had they waited longer I would have given them better evidence that my hope had a substantial foundation, but I am afraid that I could not have given them enough evidence to make them share my expectations.

The possibility of my nomination led me to urge Mrs. Bryan to attend the Convention, a precaution of which I was afterwards glad when the Convention resulted as it did. We took rooms at the Clifton House, where my delegation had headquarters.

As some comment has been made upon the fact that our delegation had rooms at the Clifton, I might explain that we tried to get rooms at the Palmer House, but all the other delegation from Nebraska had secured headquarters there, and we went to the Clifton, not so much because it was less expensive there as because it was nearer to the Palmer House than any other hotel. Our delegates were prepared to meet whatever expense was necessary, but they wanted to be near the center of political activity, and the Clifton House suited their purpose. I may add, however, that as the rates were lower at the Clifton House, I can point to a less pretentious hotel bill than I would have had at the Palmer House. I took $100 with me and after paying the hotel bill of Mrs. Bryan and myself during the Convention week I had about $40 left, a sum probably as small as anyone has spent in securing a presidential nomination. It did not, of course, include my share of the expenses of the delegates or the expenses of the preliminary contest in which the delegates were selected, but even this sum was inconsiderable, as no money whatever was spent in entertaining delegations or delegates.

My ambition had been to be chairman of the Committee on Resolutions, but I found that Senator Jones aspired to that place, and as he was a much older man, and the president of the bimetallic organization formed at Memphis, I did not care to be a candidate against him, and gave up the thought of that place. As our delegation was shut out of the temporary organization by the National Committee, it would have been impossible for me to be chairman of the Committee on Resolutions, but the committee did not act until after I had given up the idea. Then there was some talk of my being voted for as permanent chairman, but by this time the papers had begun to discuss the possibility of my being a candidate, and I was objected to by the friends of other candidates. As my time was occupied in the contest before the Credentials Committee, I did not get a chance to attend the convention during the earlier sessions, and although I was called for when others were called for, I did not have a chance to speak to the Convention.

The exclusion of my delegates was a good illustration of

machine politics. As has been shown elsewhere, there was not the slightest ground for the opposing delegates. There was irregularity in our Conventions and it represented more than nineteen-twentieths of the party vote in Nebraska. But the Gold and corporation faction had control of the old National Committee and the other delegation was seated, making us the contesting delegation before the Credentials Committee of the delegates. The delegates desired me to lead the fight before the committee and this kept me from attending the sessions of the Committee on Resolutions for which I was selected by our delegates.

The contest before the Credentials Committee of the Convention was one-sided, the opposition bringing in no minority report. I was more exultant over the seating of our delegation than I was over my nomination. In the former case I could rejoice with the boys, in the latter case my rejoicing was sobered by a sense of responsibility.

As soon as our delegation was seated, I went at once to the Committee on Resolutions, of which I was a member by selection of my delegation, and found the platform practically completed. I looked at a draft of it and found that the money plank was there as I had written it two weeks before. While in St. Louis, attending the Republican Convention, I had called upon Mr. Charles H. Jones, then editor of the *Post-Dispatch*. He was a very able man, entirely in sympathy with the progressive ideas of the party. I found him engaged in writing a draft of the platform to be presented at Chicago. I prepared a plank covering the money question and he inserted it in the platform which he was drawing.

I hasten to explain that the language which I employed was language which had been incorporated in many state planks beginning more than a year before. I explain elsewhere the origin of the most prominent plank in the platform. There was no part of the plank which had not been

108

thoroughly discussed and quite unanimously approved by the advocates of bimetallism.

When that plank was adopted by the Committee on Resolutions, it is probable that the members did not know that I had written it—at least, I have no reason to believe that they did know—and they approved of it in my absence. There were two planks which, according to my recollection, I added after I joined the committee. Some one suggested that we had no plank on arbitration and, if my memory serves me well, I wrote that plank and it was accepted. And then some suggested that there was no plank on the Venezuela question, and I wrote that plank. It will be seen, therefore, that I had very little to do with the writing of the Chicago platform, although since the Convention I have been given credit for writing it.

And now came an unexpected stroke of luck. Soon after we went into the Convention to report the platform, a page came to me and said that Senator Jones wanted to see me. I went to his seat and he asked me if I would take charge of the debate. I asked him if he did not want to conduct the debate himself and he replied in the negative. The request came as a surprise, for he had never intimated to me that he wanted me to do this, and I had never suggested it to him or anyone else.

I digress for a moment to remind the readers that this was a position to which I aspired in the beginning but for which I was not willing to be a candidate after I heard of Senator Jones' aspirations. I had seen my chance of temporary chairmanship disappear and then the chance for the permanent chairmanship—which afterward had become impossible because the possibility of my nomination made the other candidates hostile to the suggestion. And now, having passed through the circle of disappointment, I found myself in the very position for which I had at first longed.

Before continuing the narrative the reader may be interested, as I was, to know why this good fortune befell me.

After the Convention was over and Senator Jones had been made chairman of the National Committee at my request, I asked him how he happened to turn the defense of the platform over to me. I know that it was not with any thought of favoring me as a candidate, because he was a supporter of Mr. Bland and too loyal to him to have knowingly given an opportunity to any possible candidate if there was any likelihood of the opportunity being used to the disadvantage of his choice. And I myself had no thought of the effect produced by the speech. While I had, before the Convention met, regarded my nomination as a possibility I had relied upon what I called the logic of the situation rather than upon the influence of a speech.

The speech that I expected to make was not different from the speeches that I had been making except in the setting, to which I had not given special consideration. My interest was in the subject and I felt that I was master of the subject and could give expression to the sentiment of the Convention as represented by a little more than two-thirds of its members. Senator Jones answered my question by saying that I was the only one of the prominent speakers who had not had an opportunity to address the Convention. He referred to the speeches made by the temporary and permanent chairman and by others who were called out by the Convention while I was attending the meeting of the Committee on Credentials. He knew of the part I had taken in the organizing of the fight and how I had traveled over the country for a year helping in many states and said that his invitation to me was due entirely to a sense of fairness, and hence I honored him more for it than I could have done had it been due to partiality for me.

But to return to his request. I asked him what members of the committee wanted to speak on the platform and he said that no one had asked for time except Senator Tillman. I then went to Senator Hill, of New York, he was the leader of the minority, and arranged with him about the time to be allotted to the discussion. We agreed to an hour and a quarter on a side. I believe that was the time named. I then went to Senator Tillman and asked him whether he wanted to open or close the debate. He said he would like to close and that he wanted fifty minutes. I told him that that was too long for a closing speech and that I hardly thought the other side would agree to our using so much of the time in closing. I went back to Senator Hill and presented Senator Tillman's request and he objected to it, as I supposed he would, and said that if Senator Tillman wanted to use as much time as that he ought to use it in opening. I then returned to Senator Tillman and stated the case, and as he, Senator Tillman, felt that he needed more time than Senator Hill was willing to use in closing, he decided to open the debate and left me to close it. This again was an advantage, but it was an advantage that came by circumstance, for I would not have felt justified in refusing to allow Senator Tillman to close the debate if he had been willing to accept a shorter time.

I had spoken long enough to know that, comparing myself with myself, I was more effective in a brief speech in conclusion than a longer speech that simply laid down propositions for another to answer.

Fortune favored me again. For some reason—I do not now recall what the reason was—the debate on the platform was put over until the next day and I had time to think over my speech during the night and to arrange my arguments in so far as one can arrange arguments for a closing speech. I fitted my definition of the business man at the place that I thought best and kept my "cross of gold and crown of thorns" for the conclusion. When it became known that I was to have charge of the debate my delegation was quite buoyant. They had known of debates in Nebraska and they were confident that my closing speech would make an impression on the Convention.

When the Convention convened I felt as I always do

just before a speech of unusual importance. I usually have a feeling of weakness at the pit of my stomach—a suggestion of faintness. I want to lie down. But this being impossible in the Convention, I got a sandwich and a cup of coffee and devoted myself to these as I waited for the debate to begin. During these moments of suspense Clarke Howell, with whom I became acquainted in 1893 and whose father was one of the leaders in the silver movement, sent me a note scribbled on an envelope. It read, "This is a great opportunity." I wrote under the words, "You will not be disappointed," and sent the envelope back to him.

Senator Tillman's speech did not present our side to the satisfaction of the friends of bimetallism. It was a strong speech—he could not make any other kind—but it presented the question as a sectional issue between the south and west with northeast states on the other side. While that division was very clearly presented in the Convention, we did not regard it as a necessary division; we believed that the restoration of bimetallism would be beneficial to the nations everywhere, not only to this country but all over the world. When Senator Tillman was through, Senator Jones took the platform and announced to the Convention that the Committee did not endorse the sectional argument by Senator Tillman. This increased my responsibility because it threw the whole burden on my closing speech.

Senator Hill followed Senator Tillman and made a very strong speech. He was at his best and presented the arguments on his side with consummate skill and adroitness. The effect upon the audience was apparent and the nervousness of our delegation increased as he proceeded.

He was followed by Senator Vilas, a man of high standing in the party, large experience in politics, and great ability as a lawyer. He pounded the advocates of free coinage without mercy.

Near the close of his speech Governor Russell of Massachusetts, who was the third and last man on the gold side, came back to Senator Hill's seat with evident excitement and protested that Senator Vilas was not going to leave him any time. My seat was so near Senator Hill's that I could hear the conversation. I immediately stepped across the aisle to Senator Hill and suggested that I was willing to have the time extended to give Governor Russell the time he wanted, the same period to be added to my time. Governor Russell was very appreciative of the suggestion and Senator Hill at once agreed to it. I cannot say that it was entirely unselfish on my side, and I think I would have made the suggestion if the extension of time had fallen to some one else, but as it was, it added about ten minutes to my time and I needed it for the speech I was to make. This was another unexpected bit of good fortune. I had never had such an opportunity before in my life and never expect to have again.

There never was such a setting for a political speech in my own experience, and so far as I know there never was such a setting for any other political speech ever made in this country, and it must be remembered that the setting has a great deal to do with a speech. Webster says that the essentials for a successful speech are eloquence, the subject, and the occasion. I felt that I had at least two-thirds of the requirements. I had a subject of transcendent importance. The demonetization of silver in 1873 had so decreased the world's supply of standard money as to bring about a shrinkage in values that covered a period of more than twenty years. This shrinkage in prices caused by the increase in the purchasing power of the dollar had led to three international conferences in which the leading nations had sought in vain for a remedy. Many prominent Republicans were on record as in favor of remonetization as the only means of fighting for the restoration of the parity between money and property. The Republican Convention had declared for the maintenance of the gold only until it

113

was possible to restore international bimetallism by agreement and the platform pledged the party to an effort to secure international bimetallism. The cause was great enough to bring about a revolt in the Democratic Party—a fight won by the rank and file against all the power of the administration, and of the power of the big corporations and the metropolitan press. I was to make the final speech to a Convention in sympathy with our fight.

After an unsatisfactory opening of the debate and after our side had been pounded unmercifully by the giants of the other side, all that was necessary to success was to put into words the sentiments of a majority of the delegates to the Convention—to be the voice of a triumphant majority. The occasion was there and complete in every detail. I had no doubt that I could meet the expectations that had been aroused by this extraordinary combination of circumstances, because I had spent three years studying the question from every angle and I had time and again answered all the arguments that the other side had advanced. All that I had to do was to analyze the speeches of Hill, Vilas, and Russell as they were made and then present the answer as effectively as I could.

The delegates had been hammered by the very able speech of Senator Hill; they had been provoked by the language of General Vilas, and still further irritated by the speech of Governor Russell, and they were in a mood to applaud. Fortunately my voice filled the hall, and as I was perfectly familiar with the subject, I was prepared to answer in an extemporaneous speech the arguments which had been presented—that is, extemporaneous in so far as its arrangement was concerned. No new arguments had been advanced and therefore no new answers were required.

The excitement of the moment was so intense that I hurried to the platform and began at once. My nervousness left me instantly and I felt as composed as if I had been speaking to a small audience on an unimportant occasion.

114

From the first sentence the audience was with me. My voice reached to the uttermost parts of the hall, which is a great advantage in speaking to an assembly like that.

I shall never forget the scene upon which I looked. I believe it unrivaled in any convention ever held in our country. The audience seemed to rise and sit down as one man. At the close of a sentence it would rise and shout, and when I began upon another sentence, the room was as still as a church. There was inspiration in the faces of the delegates. My own delegation I can never forget. No man ever had a more loyal sixteen friends than I had on that day. Their faces glowed with enthusiasm.

Two faces stand out as in memory I look over the hall. Ex-Governor Hogg, of Texas, was a large man, probably six feet two or three inches in height, and heavy. He wore no beard and his face was beaming with delight. He stood by the aisle to my left, and about in the same relative position on my right stood Ollie James, a member from Kentucky, also a large man with a smooth face. As I turned from one side of the hall to the other, these two faces impressed me, for like the rest of the audience, they were in full sympathy with the sentiments to which I gave expression. They could not have responded to the expressions of my own face more perfectly if I had been speaking a speech that they had prepared.

The audience acted like a trained choir—in fact, I thought of a choir as I noted how instantaneously and in unison they responded to each point made.

The situation was so unique and the experience so unprecedented that I have never expected to witness its counterpart.

At the conclusion of my speech the demonstration spread over nearly the entire convention. As is customary at such times, the standards of the various states were carried through the aisles followed by the delegates, the Nebraska standard at the front. During the demonstration many persons came to me to tell me of the votes in their delegations; in some cases whole states were pledged. Others came to ask questions.

I remember that one man came to report that I was accused of drinking to excess. It was easy to answer him with the assurance that I was and always had been a tee-totaler. Another man came to tell me that some one in his delegation accused me of saying that I would not support a gold candidate if one were nominated by our convention. I replied that I had stated that I would no more support a gold standard or a gold platform than I would an army marching on my home. The delegate said that he would not either and went back to carry my answer.

After the nomination Hon. Arthur Sewall, my running mate, came to tell me of an experience which in the confusion had made no impression upon me. He said that he came up and told me that they would nominate me that night if my friends would prevent adjournment. He quoted me as answering, "Should I want to be nominated tonight if they would be sorry for it tomorrow?"

To another, as he reported to me afterwards, I said, "If the desire to nominate me will not last until tomorrow, would it last during the campaign?"

The nomination came on the following day on the fifth ballot. I had been so busy all the forenoon that I had not had time to shave. When the bulletin was brought in announcing my nomination I knew that the crowd would soon turn from the Convention to my headquarters, and I hurried down to the barber for a shave. I mention this as evidence that I was not excited, but the barber was—so much so that he could hardly handle his razor.

Mr. Sewall, who became my running mate, was one of the first to call to congratulate me. When they met for the selection of Vice-President I sent for some of the leaders and told them that I had no choice for that position and did not care to advise further than to say that I had no objection to the nomination of a Southern man if the Convention thought proper to do so. I did not mean to advise such a nomination, but I wanted them to know that I did not share the objection so often raised to a Southern man. I felt then, as I have felt since, that a man otherwise eligible should not be barred because he lived in the South, even though he were an ex-Confederate, as most of the men old enough to be candidates were. I had become convinced, even then, that the voters were not so much interested in the locality of the candidate or in his position during the Civil War as they were in his attitude on public questions.

Honorable Arthur Sewall was nominated, the chief argument being that I lived so far West that they should have an Eastern man to balance the ticket. Mr. Sewall had gained distinction as the only silver man on the National Committee representing eastern states. He had voted to seat the Nebraska delegation when the question was before the committee. I did not know Mr. Sewall until he was nominated, but I learned to love him as I became acquainted with him. I soon learned that he was a thorough Democrat. I sounded him along the various lines and never in a single instance did I find him holding views inconsistent with the most fundamental Democracy. He was a well-to-do man but a believer in the Income Tax; he was a national banker but preferred the Government note to the bank note. His sympathies were with the common people and he was true to their interests on every subject. Because of Mr. Watson's nomination by the Populist Convention, Mr. Sewall did not take an active part in the campaign. Had he made speeches I am sure that he would have become more popular in the West than in the East, because his views were entirely in harmony with the sentiment in those sections that dominated the Convention.

This word in behalf of Mr. Sewall is due to him. I can never forget the last time that I met him. I was speaking in the South when he happened to be near where I was to speak. He wired me inquiring the time of my train, and learning that I would pass over a certain road, he met me. He appeared with me on the platform at several points where crowds were gathered, and just as he was leaving me at a place where quite an enthusiastic crowd was gathered, he said with tears in his eyes, as he bade me good-by, "Mr. Bryan, how these people love you," and I am sure that they loved me no better than Mr. Sewall did, and his affection was reciprocated by me.

The Convention closed on Saturday and Mrs. Bryan and I spent Sunday with the family of Judge Lyman Trumbull, who had died a short time before the Convention. Then came the trip to Lincoln by way of Salem, my birthplace, where we had left the children while we went to attend the Convention.

This is the story of my connection with the Convention that has had such an important influence upon my public life. I put it in writing at this time so that the story will not be lost in case my life should be ended before I have time to prepare a more detailed sketch.

In speaking of the Convention it has been my purpose to record only the incidents that were personal and of which others would have less knowledge than I. I prefer to let disinterested parties describe the impression made by the speech and the demonstration.

CHAPTER VII

LEADING UP TO MY SECOND NOMINATION

THE number of letters which I received after the election of 1896 made it certain that unless some change in conditions occurred, I would be renominated in 1900, for although defeated, the six and a half millions of voters came out of the campaign of 1896 a compact and undismayed army. The elections of 1897 indicated a growth in our party's strength and things went well until the Spanish War broke out, then attention was turned from economic matters to questions affecting the war.

I telegraphed to President McKinley on the day that the war was declared offering my services, but never received a reply. I know that the telegram was received, because the President asked Senator Allen, of Nebraska, what position I could fill, and Senator Allen communicated the question to me. I wrote the Senator that I was willing to do any work to which I might be assigned, but suggested that as I was personally acquainted with General Wheeler, it would be agreeable to be assigned to his staff if the rules permitted. Senator Allen did not receive my letter until after General Wheeler had gone South, and I afterwards learned that the rules of the army would have prevented my being assigned to his staff, as I was not a commissioned officer and had had no experience. Shortly afterwards Governor Holcomb, of Nebraska, authorized me to raise a regiment—I had already enlisted as a private in a company organized at Lincoln. I raised the regiment and served something more than five months, resigned the day that the treaty with Spain was signed, so that my military career began constructively with the offer of my services on the day that war was declared, and with the termination of my services on the day that the war was formally closed by treaty.

During my army life I refused all social invitations and attended strictly to the duties of the office. I also avoided any discussion of political questions, giving as an excuse that I had military lockjaw. After I began to recruit a regiment, but before I was sworn in, I had occasion to make a speech at a dinner in Omaha, where the subject of imperialism was approached, and I then announced my opposition to colonialism, and so far as I know, I was the first public man to express myself on this subject. Ex-President Cleveland and Senator Hoar, according to my recollection, made speeches, or gave interviews, a few days afterwards along the same line.

My reason for leaving the army was that I saw that the sentiment in favor of imperialism was widespread and that many Democrats had been led to join in the cry for expansion, as it was then termed. I believed imperialism to be dangerous to the country, and so believing, I resigned my position in the army in order to oppose it. It required more courage to resign than it did to enlist, for I knew that the unfriendly papers would criticise me for leaving the army just as they had criticised me for entering it. They stated that, having no military experience, I was not fit to take charge of a regiment and that it was unfair to the soldiers in my regiment to be under my command. When I resigned they stated that I had deserted my soldiers and that it was unfair to the soldiers for me to leave them while they were still in service.

When I left the army the question before the country was the ratification of the treaty, and I announced the next day after I put on citizen's clothes that I favored the ratification of the treaty and the declaration of the nation's purpose to give independence to the Filipinos. As my reason for taking this position has been explained and defended in my speech on imperialism made when I accepted the nomination in 1900 (see Chapter XXI), I need not set forth this reason here.   I have never regretted the position taken; on the contrary, I never showed more statesmanship than I did when I insisted upon the termination of the war and the making of the promise embodied in the Bacon resolution.

The Democratic party was in the minority in the Senate and in the House, and a Republican President was in the White House.   Our party, therefore, could not pass a resolution through either body, and it had no voice in the selection of the treaty commissioners.   It required two thirds of the Senate to confirm the treaty, and a few Republicans were willing to act with the Democrats to reject it.

But the Republicans and Democrats stood in different positions.   The Democrats had to furnish the bulk of the votes to reject the treaty, and had no influence with the administration.   The Republicans who opposed the treaty were few in number but hoped that, through their influence with the administration, they might be able to modify the terms of the treaty.   But the Democrats would have had to have borne the responsibility for the continuation of war expenditures and for any dangers that arose during the continuation of the state of war.   Hostilities were feared and parents were clamoring for the return of their sons, and it was difficult for Democrats to defend an act that would continue the state of war and postpone the making of the treaty.

Then, too, several of the great nations of Europe, such as England, Germany, and Russia, were interested in the Orient and might resent the setting up of a republic there. England was not interested in the spread of the ideas of popular government in India, neither was Germany interested in having colonies take up the ideas of self-government, and Russia was at that time the most despotic of the European empires.   If we had insisted upon the recognition of the independence of the Philippine republic, it might have brought us into conflict with the interests of several

European powers, and it was not necessary for us to take this risk because we could give independence to the Filipinos more easily than we could force Spain to give independence. By ratifying the treaty, we settled the question with Spain and gave to ourselves the entire control of the Philippine situation.

It then became an easy matter for us to make to the Filipinos the same promise that the treaty made to the Cubans. The ratification of the treaty did not bind us to hold the Philippine Islands; it simply severed the Philippine Islands from Spain. I felt confident that it was easier to persuade the American people to promise independence to the Filipinos in connection with the ratification of the treaty than to continue war and force Spain to recognize a republic in the Philippines. I still believe that we followed the line of least responsibility and that we are better off today for having settled the war and made the Philippine question purely an American question than we would have been had we, a minority in Congress, attempted to compel a majority to carry out a plan by which the majority would in turn be compelled to force Spain to recognize the independence of the Philippine republic.

The Bacon resolution, which was a part of my plan, came so near being adopted that it required the vote of the Vice-President to defeat it. It will be seen, therefore, that although I was a private citizen, the Senate came within one vote of carrying out a plan which I had outlined and for which I had been severely criticised. Had the plan been carried out, we would have been saved the tremendous expense which has followed our attempt at colonialism and we would have been spared the menace to which our meddling in Oriental politics has subjected us.

For a while the excitement regarding expansion, as the Republicans termed it, and imperialism, as we termed it, aroused suggestions as to other candidates. Admiral Dewey was spoken of and even went so far as to indicate his willingness to accept the nomination, although he did not indicate with which party he expected to connect himself. Admiral Schley was also spoken of as a candidate, but refused to consider the matter.

As the convention of 1900 approached, however, it became evident that no other candidate would be presented to the convention, and when the convention was held, the delegates from all of the states and territories but one, if my memory is correct, were instructed to favor my nomination. It is possible that two or three of the states instead of instructing, passed resolutions expressing a preference for me. When the convention met at Kansas City, I was not present. Mr. R. L. Metcalfe, editor of the *World-Herald*, and a delegate at large, was the Nebraska member of the Committee on Resolutions.

Mr. C. H. Jones, who prepared the draft of the Chicago platform, had prepared the draft of the Kansas City platform, using very largely the phraseology that I had employed in the discussion of the questions. About the only plank that aroused discussion was the plank restating the Chicago platform for the restoration of bimetallism and the opening of the mints to the free coinage of silver at the ratio of sixteen to one. The Eastern delegates were opposed to the restatement of this proposition, although they were willing to reaffirm the platform as a whole without any special reference to this plank. As it was intended, however, to restate nearly all the other planks of the Chicago platform, it was evident that the failure to restate this plank was equivalent to a repudiation of it, notwithstanding the general endorsement of the Chicago platform as a whole. I insisted upon the restatement of the plank because I thought that a refusal to restate it would, under the circumstances, be considered a repudiation of that plank, and while I recognized the force of the arguments made by some of our friends, namely, that the increased production of gold since 1896 had reduced the importance of the question, I was not willing to run upon a platform which either ignored the question or put me in the attitude of pretending to endorse it when the endorsement was not genuine.

I considered the matter very fully, and nothing ever distressed me more than being compelled to differ from so many of my trusted friends. A number of those who had been loyal to me in the former campaign were persuaded by the arguments of the Eastern delegates who favored the reaffirmation of the platform without a specific restatement of this plank, and but for my objection, the resolutions committee would have so acted. Even with my objection known, the vote in the committee was quite close. Several friends sent a representative to Lincoln to ask me to leave the question of the platform to the convention, and I replied that I would gladly do so, but when asked if I would be a candidate in case the convention decided to leave out that plank, I replied that I would not consent to be a candidate under those circumstances. I had fought for four years for the reaffirmation of that platform and I was not willing to go before the country on a deceptive promise, as I felt it would be a deceptive promise if the convention merely reaffirmed but refused to reiterate.

I told the friends there that I could afford to lose the nomination, that it was not necessary to my happiness, but that I could not afford to lose the confidence that the voters had in my honesty and that I would decline to be a candidate if the convention in its wisdom saw fit to write the platform as was then proposed. So unwilling was I to put my judgment against the judgment of the committee that I was on the point of sending a communication to the convention declining to be a candidate under any circumstance, for I felt that the support of the convention would not be a hearty support if it approved of a platform against its own judgment, and yet I was not willing to be a candidate under conditions that required me to apologize for the platform.

MY SECOND NOMINATION

I was prevented from sending this communication by the fact that the delegates were instructed for me and that it was not the fault of those who gave the instructions that the delegates were considering the propriety of yielding to the demand that came from the East. Some have thought that my refusal to consent to this change in the platform resulted in my defeat, but I have never entertained this view of the subject. I believe that the acceptance of the modified platform would have resulted in a more disastrous defeat than the one which I suffered. In fact I believe that had I consented to run on such a platform, I would have so disappointed the rank and file who made the fight for me in 1896 that I would have had something of the experience that Mr. Parker had four years later.

I did agree to the plank making imperialism the paramount issue, because I believed that with changed conditions the question of imperialism was at that time more important than the money question. The trust plank was given the second place in importance, and the money question was not discussed to any extent during the campaign. The fact that the platform reiterated the demand for independent bimetallism made it less necessary for me to discuss the question than it would have been had the platform attempted to avoid the subject. As it was, the substitution of imperialism as the paramount issue discouraged a great many of our active workers, and while I gained in the New England states and in what used to be called the middle states, those in the neighborhood of New York, I lost in the South, in the Mississippi Valley states and in the West.

A word more in regard to the contest in the committee at Kansas City. I was in telephonic communication with friends at Kansas City, and the Kansas City *Times* was being edited by a close political friend who sent a representative to Lincoln, with whom I was to confer, and it was willing to carry out editorially any suggestions that I should make. The resolutions committee harangued over the platform far into the night and as the time approached for the paper to go to press, the editor sent his representative to me to get an indication of the outcome in case the committee rejected what was known as my plank. I told him that the paper could safely have an editorial written upon the assumption that I would not be a candidate in case the convention rejected that plank. I did not tell him so, but I had no thought of letting the fight drop with a mere resolution of the committee. I would have gone to Kansas City if necessary and made a fight in the convention for an adoption of the plank; if the convention had then rejected the plank, I then would not have been a candidate.

The committee, however, by a very small majority, declared in favor of the plank, and no minority report was filed. It has sometimes been stated that the vote of the delegate from Hawaii decided the result in the committee. If so, it might be interesting to know that a Democrat passed through Lincoln years before on his way to Hawaii and asked me for a letter of introduction to President Dole. The man brought with him a letter from a friend which contained a sufficient endorsement to justify me in giving the letter desired. I saw nothing more of the man until after the Kansas City convention. When I learned that he was present at Kansas City and that he made it his business to advise the Hawaii member of the Committee on Resolutions and to fortify him against the persuasion that came from the opposition, I did not know, of course, to what extent his loyalty may have influenced the vote of the Hawaiian member, but if it did have influence, it is another evidence that bread cast upon the waters may return after many days, for it was a favorable return that this man made for the slight service that I rendered him in giving him a letter of introduction.

It ought also to be known that Mr. Richard Croker, the leader of Tammany, played an important part in this matter. Mr. Croker met with an accident a little while before the

MY SECOND NOMINATION

Kansas City Convention, and while he was laid up by the accident, he read my book entitled "The First Battle." The arguments in favor of silver convinced him of the correctness of our position, or at least removed the prejudice he had against our position. When he came back from his trip abroad he announced that he was in favor of my nomination and he sent me word that he would support the platform that I wanted. When New York's member of the resolution committee was to be selected, Mr. Croker favored Judge Van Wyck in place of Senator Hill, and he did so because he was afraid to trust Senator Hill on that question. Mr. Van Wyck voted against my plank on the committee. I have always believed that he would have voted with me had his vote been necessary—but he refused to join in any minority report. As soon as it became known that the committee had included the plank for which I asked, Senator Hill began an agitation in favor of a minority report, and I was informed at the time that Mr. Croker, upon learning of it, notified Mr. Hill that New York's votes would be cast in favor of the majority report. This ended the fight and the platform was unanimously adopted. Mr. Croker was an enthusiastic supporter during the campaign, and after the election wrote me a letter expressing his regret at my defeat and saying that he still expected me to be elected to the presidency. He was one of the few Eastern Democrats who wrote me after the election. I have appreciated Mr. Croker's support of me because I believed it entirely disinterested. He never asked a promise of me; never said anything to indicate that he had any personal reason for favoring me, and I have every reason to believe that he stated his real reason for supporting me when he gave as his reason that he believed that I was in public life because of my interest in the public and not because I had any pecuniary advantage in view.

Hon. A. E. Stephenson was nominated for Vice-President at Kansas City and his nomination was entirely satisfactory.

127

WILLIAM JENNINGS BRYAN

He is a man of splendid character and was faithful to the core in 1896 when the President and nearly all of his prominent appointees deserted the party. I explained to General Stephenson that if elected I would ask congress to enact a law to make the Vice-President ex-officio member of the cabinet in order that he might be present at all consultations and be fully informed as to all administration plans. Such a law I think would add dignity to the office of Vice-President and at the same time prepare the Vice-President for the better discharge of the duties of the office in case of the President's death. I had resolved on this recommendation as far back as 1896 and may have spoken to Mr. Sewall of it, but am not sure about it. The matter had so impressed me that the first issue of the *Commoner* contained an editorial on the subject.

CHAPTER VIII

THE BENNETT WILL CASE

THE friendship between Philo S. Bennett and myself, which began in 1896 and continued until his death, was one of my closest and dearest friendships outside of my family, and yet it brought upon me an experience which gave rise to more malicious misrepresentation than any other incident of my life. It was the only time in which I have been called upon to serve a friend at great expense to myself both in feelings and in money. I am glad to put upon permanent record the facts in connection with it. It is now possible to discuss the case with more freedom than was possible during the lifetime of Mrs. Bennett.

Philo S. Bennett was a citizen of New Haven, Connecticut, but was engaged in business in the city of New York. His firm, Bennett, Sloan & Company, were wholesale grocers, specializing in tea.

I never met Mr. Bennett until the campaign of 1896, when he was on the reception committee on the occasion of my campaign visit to New Haven.

Speaking some six hundred times during the campaign, it was of course impossible for me to recall the members of all the reception committees which took part in meetings. It so happened that at New Haven, Connecticut, Mr. Bennett rode in the carriage with me along with John B. Sargent, a prominent hardware manufacturer of that city. I had known of Mr. Sargent for some years, because he was one of the few Eastern manufacturers opposed to a protective tariff. He had made a trip around the world and on his return gained a considerable prominence by interviews in which he declared that American manufacturers could compete with the world without a tariff; basing his arguments on observations he made as a traveler. The proposition that I remember best was that American labor was so much more efficient than foreign labor that our power to compete in the markets of the world increased as the percentage of skilled labor in the manufactured articles increased. Mr. Sargent's name had therefore become known to me and I remembered the personal meeting with him and the support which he gave to our cause, but would not have been able to remember Mr. Bennett but for our correspondence which brought him to my attention just before the election. The following letter is the first which I received from him:

BENNETT, SLOAN & Co.

New York, October 30, 1896.

Hon. William J. Bryan
Lincoln, Neb.
DEAR SIR:

The betting is three to one against you in this state at the present time; but notwithstanding that, I am impressed with a feeling that you will win, and if you are *defeated*, I wish to make you a gift of $3,000; and if you will accept the same it will be a genuine pleasure to me to hand it to you any time after the 10th of next March.

You have made one of the most gallant fights on record for a principle, against the combined money power of the whole country, and if you are not successful now, you will be, in my opinion, four years later.

The solid press of the East, and all the wealth of the country have, ever since the canvass opened, concealed the truth and deceived the people regarding the whole question. They have succeeded in making 25 per cent of them believe that if you are elected the country will be governed by a lawless, disorganized mob. If you are elected I trust that you will, as soon as you can, issue a letter or make a speech, assuring them that the great body of the people are honest and can be trusted.

This letter is intended only for yourself and wife to ever see. A feeling of gratitude for what you have done in this canvass for humanity, for right and justice, prompts me to write and make this offer.

I am one of the electors at large on the silver ticket in the state of Connecticut, and accompanied you from New York to New Haven, and rode in the carriage with you and Mr. Sargent from the station to the hotel.

Hoping for your victory, and with kind regards, I am,

Sincerely yours,

P. S. Bennett.

Mr. Bennett's first letter indicated such a sympathetic interest in our party's position on public questions that our acquaintance grew. It became more intimate as I met him from time to time on my trips to the East, and our friendship continued unbroken until his accidental death in 1903. I seldom passed through New York without seeing him. He invited Mrs. Bryan and me to spend a summer vacation with him and Mrs. Bennett at their summer home in Maine, but it was never possible to accept his invitation except as we met him for a day or two in New York or New Haven. He was so much older than I that the relationship between us was more like the relation between parent and child, he giving me the benefit of his greater experience and larger business acquaintance.

It will be noticed that this letter was written just before the election and the offer contained in it was contingent upon my defeat. The letter did not come to my attention until after the election, by which time I discovered that the campaign had brought upon me a continuing expense in the way of correspondence. The number of letters received amounted to twenty-five hundred or sometimes three thousand a day. It soon became apparent that my correspondence would cost me more than it ever cost me to live before I was nominated. Mr. Bennett's offer, coming at such a time, was quite welcome, but before accepting it I took the precaution to inquire by letter addressed directly to him whether he was pecuniarily interested in silver mining. Believing that the silver question would continue to be an issue, I was not willing to put myself under financial obligation to anyone who was in a business way interested in silver as a metal. My interest in silver was solely as a matter of the public interests; the demonetization of silver seemed at that time the only way of increasing the volume of money.

I quote from his reply dated November 20, 1896:

New York, Nov. 20, 1896.

Hon. William J. Bryan,
    Lincoln, Neb.
DEAR SIR:

I have yours dated the 13th inst. I do not now, and never have owned a dollar's interest in a silver, gold or any other mine, and do not expect to in this century.

If just as agreeable to you, I will make the gift in three different payments, sending you check for $1,000 the 15th of each March for the next three years.

I would like to have you use it all for yourself and family, and not give a penny for the cause of silver or any other political purpose.

The newspapers report that you are to enter the lecture field. If this is true, when you go to New Haven it would afford me pleasure to entertain you while there. I am confident you will have a full house and be received enthusiastically.

I am anxious to have you seen and heard on the platform in the East by the gold advocates, for I think it will help to remove from their minds some of the prejudice that now exists. To me it seems one of the best methods you have open for that purpose; it will also help hold your old friends.

You of course fully understand the *power of money and brains coupled together.* You may rest assured that both will be used lavishly to prevent you from securing the nomination for President in 1900. From now on if you mingle and keep in touch with the people, I believe they will remain true, and you can secure the nomination against the all-powerful forces named.

I hope that before 1900 you will in some manner gain the support and goodwill of part of the business element. Here in the East and middle states they were almost solid against you in November. It is important that you should have it next time in order to carry any electoral votes in this part of the country, for the money power, as it is generally understood, will be a unit against you.

I have just received the Boston *Herald*, containing a speech by Mr. F. A. Walker on bimetallism, delivered on the 7th inst.

I suppose you know that Mr. Walker has his eye on the presidency, and hopes to secure the nomination some time from the friends of bimetallism. Keep close watch on him. After reading his speech I will forward it to you.

I send you a few clippings which you will probably feel interested in reading.

With kind regards, I am,

Sincerely yours,

P. S. BENNETT.

Perhaps I ought to qualify what I have said about Gen. Walker, for I have no *positive* knowledge that he expects the nomination.

In April or May of 1900 I received a letter from Mr. Bennett asking whether I would be home at a certain time in the near future, without giving me any intimation of the object of his proposed visit. Upon receiving my answer in the affirmative, he appeared one morning at our home in Nebraska. He laid before me a will which he had made some years before, stating that he desired to make some changes in it.

He said that he felt as much interested in the reforms which I was advocating as I did myself, but that he was unable to present them to the public as I was in the habit of doing. It had occurred to him that if he made provision in his will for a sum that would be given to me at his death I would be able to make, without compensation, speeches that I delivered in the form of lectures, and he desired to set apart fifty thousand dollars for that purpose, saying that he would leave ten thousand dollars in care of Mrs. Bryan, five thousand dollars to each of my children and twenty-five thousand to myself. He felt that in this way he could share in the work and would feel that he was making a contribution that was within his means.

I inquired whether he would have that sum to spare after making provision for his wife and relatives. He told me that he was worth about three hundred thousand dollars, and that he was giving one hundred thousand to his wife, a sum which he said would furnish her a larger income than she could use during the remainder of her life. They had no children, their only child, a daughter, having died some years before. They lived comfortably but without ostentation and they had estimated the amount necessary to provide for all the wants of his wife should she be left a widow. He went further and explained that the money which he left her would at her death go to her relatives and the amount he was allotting to her was all he cared to leave them. The amount he left to his own relatives, a sister and a half brother, had been decided by him without any consultation with me.

In fact, he did not consult with me about any item of

134

the will except that fifty thousand dollars which he wanted to give to me and thirty thousand dollars which he desired to devote to altruistic purposes. I ventured to call his attention to the fact that after giving to his wife and his relatives the amounts he desired left them and after giving fifty thousand to me, there still remained thirty thousand dollars of his estate. We talked over the various uses which could be made of this. In the course of the conversation I told him that I had established prizes in nineteen colleges, nearly all of them state universities. These prizes were given each year for the best essay on the science of government; my plan being to give two hundred fifty dollars to the institution, the interest from which would be used to furnish annual prize money. The plan pleased him and he decided to leave ten thousand to me in trust for this purpose. I was to select twenty state universities which I had not myself endowed, giving to each five hundred dollars for the purpose outlined above. That left twenty thousand dollars and Mr. Bennett expressed a desire to use it to aid poor boys and girls to secure an education, explaining that he himself had lacked educational opportunities when he was young and that it would give him satisfaction to aid those similarly situated. I discussed with him how this might be done and he asked whether I would be willing to distribute ten thousand for the aid of boys and Mrs. Bryan a similar amount for the aid of girls. He remarked that her wide acquaintance would enable her to distribute the money over the United States to the best possible advantage. These provisions were written into the will. He had a small sum left and I told him of a plan that I had in mind to buy the ground upon which I was born and upon it build a city library.

He had so impressed me by his devotion to the political ideals and principles with which I had been identified that I told him it would be very pleasant to me to have his name linked with mine in this library. The plan appealed to him and the provision was made. The library has been built and is known as "The Bryan-Bennett Library." We contributed equally to the cost of the building, but I had previously bought the land and subsequently contributed five hundred dollars for the purchase of books.

When we came to consider the fifty thousand dollars to be left to myself, I told him that I was not an old man and was likely to live for many years and that I would not promise to accept the money at the time of his death because I might not need it at the time. There was so little opposition to my second nomination that it seemed quite certain that I would run again and I told him that if I was elected I would be in a position where I would not need any financial assistance. He thought I would need the money more in case of my election than my defeat. I had no desire to accumulate means beyond a provision against old age and I preferred to have him give the money to his wife, with instructions to give it to me if at the time of his death I desired it. He preferred to give it to me directly and asked me whether I would be willing to distribute it in case I did not desire to accept it, reminding me again that he had made what he regarded as ample provision for the members of his family and wanted this sum devoted to the public. He said it gave him pleasure to contemplate the benefit which his bequest would bring to other young people, situated as he himself had been in his youth.

He insisted that I should distribute the fifty thousand dollars among charities and educational institutions if for any reason I refused to accept it. Having no thought of the possibility of a contest, I promised to do this, and it was this promise that compelled me to oppose the breaking of the will.

The money was left to his wife in trust, the terms of which would be made known to her in a letter deposited with the will.

I have gone into this in detail because the alternative

136

obligation which he imposed upon me was the matter that embarrassed me at the time of his death. He explained to me that he had given to his wife all that she could use and his estimate was borne out by subsequent facts. He left his wife about one hundred thousand dollars. When she died in 1919 she left an estate of one hundred thirty-six thousand dollars. It shows an increase rather than a diminution of the amount left her.

Mrs. Bryan, who at that time used the typewriter and helped me with a considerable part of my correspondence, copied the will at Mr. Bennett's request.

When the new will was drafted, being, as I have said, a copy of the old will except as to the five bequests above mentioned, he took it back to New York with him unsigned; then, fifteen hundred miles away from Nebraska and several days after the drawing of it, he executed the will and put it in a safety deposit vault of his own selection and of which he only had the key, notifying me of what he had done. There the will lay until his death more than three years later. The will was never mentioned in any conversation between us and never referred to in any letters. And I did not know at the time of his death whether the will was in existence.

In one of his letters written upon a wedding anniversary he remarked that he was almost old enough to be my father, adding that I could not be nearer to him if I were indeed his son. I mention this because while it made no reference to the will when he thus expressed himself, he may have had in mind the provision of his will.

Between the making of the will and his death I saw him frequently and heard from him from time to time. In the fall of 1903 he made a trip to Idaho, and arranged to stop at Lincoln on his way west. It so happened that I was away from home, so that I missed an opportunity to have what would have been a farewell visit with him. He expressed himself as greatly pleased with Fairview, our country home.   It was on this trip that he met his death by accident at a point near Boise, Idaho.   He was riding in the open stage coach commonly used on the mountain roads when the brake broke on a hill and the team became unmanageable.   He was thrown from the coach, striking against a tree, and died instantly.   His widow wired me and I went to New Haven to attend the funeral.   She greeted me affectionately, put the flowers which I brought on the coffin with her own flowers and invited me to speak at the grave, which I did.   Below will be found my remarks.

"At another time I shall take occasion to speak of the life of Philo Sherman Bennett and to draw some lessons from his career; today I must content myself with offering a word of comfort to those who knew him as husband, brother, relative, or friend—and as a friend I need a share of this comfort for myself.   It is sad enough to consign to the dust the body of one we love— how infinitely more sad if we were compelled to part with the spirit that animated this tenement of clay. But the best of man does not perish.   We bury the brain that planned for others as well as for its master, the tongue that spoke words of love and encouragement, the hands that were extended to those who needed help and the feet that ran where duty directed, but the spirit that dominated and controlled all rises triumphant over the grave.   We lay away the implements with which he wrought, but the gentle, modest, patient, sympathetic, loyal, brave and manly man whom we knew is not dead, and cannot die.   It would be unfair to count the loss of his departure without counting the gain of his existence. The gift of his life we have and of this the tomb cannot deprive us.   Separation, sudden and distressing as it is, cannot take from the companion of his life the recollection of forty years of affection, tenderness and confidence, nor from others the memory of helpful association with him. If the sunshine which a baby brings into a home, even if its sojourn is brief, cannot be dimmed by its death; if a child growing to manhood or womanhood brings to the parents a development of heart and head that outweighs any grief that its demise can cause, how much more does a long life full of kindly deeds leave us indebted to the Father who both gives and takes away. The night of death makes us remember with gratitude the light of the day that has gone while we look forward to the morning.

"The impress made by the life is lasting. We think it wonderful that we can by means of the telephone or the telegraph talk to those who are many miles away, but the achievements of the heart are even more wonderful, for the heart that gives inspiration to another heart influences all the generations yet to come. What finite mind, then, can measure the influence of a life that touched so many lives as did our friend's?

"To the young, death is an appalling thing, but it ought not to be to those whose advancing years warn them of its certain approach. As we journey along life's road we must pause again and again to bid farewell to some fellow traveler. In the course of nature the father and the mother die, then brothers and sisters follow, and finally the children and the children's children cross to the unknown world beyond—one by one 'from love's shining circle the gems drop away' until the 'king of terrors' loses his power to affright us and the increasing company on the farther shore make us first willing and then anxious to join them. It is God's way. It is God's way."

After the funeral I talked with her at her home and told her about the will drawn at my house about three and a half years previously. I told her I did not know where the will was and had no knowledge of what had occurred since and therefore did not know whether it was still in existence, but I told her of the bequests as I recalled them. She made no objection whatever to the bequest to me, but did express surprise and dissatisfaction with two other items in the will. The will as drawn made his partner, Mr. Sloan, and myself executors. I had an imperative engagement which took me away from New Haven for a few days and when I returned to present the will for probate I found that she and the other residuary legatees had employed a lawyer and decided to contest the fifty thousand dollars willed to myself.

I explained to her and to her attorneys that I would not receive any of the money for myself without her approval, but that having promised Mr. Bennett to distribute the sum if I did not receive it, I could not refuse to carry out his directions unless relieved by the court. The will was not contested on the ground that any improper influence had been brought to bear upon him, but merely on the technical ground that the provision to Mrs. Bennett did not sufficiently define the trust according to the Connecticut statute regulating wills. If the money had been given to me directly there would have been no contest and if I had not promised to distribute the sum in case I refused to accept it, I would have immediately relinquished all claims. However, having been taken into Mr. Bennett's confidence and having learned the disposition he wanted made of it, I did not feel at liberty to consult my own pleasure or my own interest.

My position was made plain to the probate judge, the circuit court and to the supreme court, so that it was known to all that I had no personal interest in the result of the suit but was simply carrying out the wishes of a dead friend. I received the most courteous treatment from all the officials who took part in the case. I employed Judge Henry G. Newton, a prominent member of the bar, to represent the estate in the defense of the will. At one time in the trial he interposed objections to an improper question and I asked him to make no objections to any questions that Mrs. Bennett's counsel might desire to ask, whether proper or not. I was not willing that any limit whatever should be placed upon interrogations, feeling that any objections might be open to misconstruction. At the conclusion of the hearing Judge Cleveland expressed himself very strongly as to the impression made by my testimony.

In the course of his written opinion, the judge said: "This court finds that neither the twelfth clause of the will (which was the clause in question) nor the letter therein referred to, was procured by undue influence." And the judge, in his written comment on the testimony, said:

"The testimony of Mr. Dewell, who had known him for a quarter of a century, shows that the testator was a sharp, able business man, a man of decided opinions from which he was not easily turned aside. But whatever presumption, if any, might be raised by reason of Mr. Bryan's drafting the will, has been, in the opinion of the court, abundantly overcome by the evidence. Mr. Bryan testifies that the idea of a bequest in his favor, so far from being suggested by him or Mrs. Bryan, was a complete surprise to both; a statement in which the court has entire confidence in view of Mr. Bryan's frankness on the witness stand and his evident desire to fully disclose all his relations with the testator and all the circumstances surrounding the drafting of the will.

The three $10,000 funds left in trust to me were distributed as follows:

BENNETT PRIZE FUND

Delaware College, Newark, Del.	$400
Bowdoin College, Brunswick, Me.	400
A. and M. College of Kentucky, Lexington, Ky.	400

Harvard University, Cambridge, Mass..............	$400
Dartmouth College, Hanover, N. H................	400
University of Tennessee, Knoxville, Tenn..........	400
St. John's College, Annapolis, Md................	400
University of Idaho, Moscow, Idaho..............	400
University of Montana, Missoula, Mont............	400
University of Utah, Salt Lake City, Utah..........	400
University of Washington, Seattle, Wash..........	400
University of South Dakota, Vermilion, S. D.......	400
University of California, Berkeley, Calif...........	400
Nevada State University, Reno, Nev..............	400
University of Colorado, Boulder, Colo.............	400
South Carolina College, Columbia, S. C..........	400
Cornell University, Ithaca, N. Y.................	400
University of Wyoming, Laramie, Wyo............	400
University of Vermont, Burlington, Vt............	400
University of Oregon, Eugene, Ore...............	400
Yale University, New Haven, Conn...............	400
Brown University, Providence, R. I..............	400
University of North Dakota, Grand Forks, N. D.....	400
University of Pennsylvania, Philadelphia, Pa.......	400
Princeton University, Princeton, N. J.............	400

Each college is to invest the amount received and use the annual income for a prize for the best essay discussing the principles of free government. I had already established similar prizes in nineteen states and the twenty-five colleges selected for the Bennett prize were selected from other states so that every state but one now contains a college giving such a prize.

EDUCATIONAL FUND FOR BOYS

The fund for the aid of poor boys desiring a college education was distributed as follows:

Illinois College, Jacksonville, Ill.................	$1,000
Park College, Parkville, Mo.....................	750

College of William and Mary, Williamsburg, Va.....	$750
Doane College, Crete, Neb......................	500
Howard College, East Lake (near Birmingham, Alabama)...............................	500
Hendrix College, Conway, Ark....................	500
Tuskegee Normal and Industrial Institute, Tuskegee, Ala.......................................	500
Kenyon College, Gambier, Ohio..................	500
Muskingum College, New Concord, Ohio...........	500
St. Olaf College, Northfield, Minn................	500
Hillsdale College, Conway, Ark..................	500
University of the South, Sewanee, Tenn............	500
Trinity University, Waxahachie, Tex..............	500
Ripon College, Ripon, Wis.......................	500
Nazareth College, Muskogee, I. T.................	500
Hope College, Holland, Mich....................	500
Butler College, Indianapolis, Ind.................	500
Sutherland College, Sutherland, Fla...............	500

Educational Fund for Girls

The fund for the aid of poor girls desiring to obtain a college education was distributed by Mrs. Bryan as follows:

Georgia Normal and Industrial College, Milledgeville, Ga...	$500
Eureka College, Eureka, Ill......................	500
Hastings College, Hastings, Neb..................	500
Wesleyan University, Buchannon, W. Va...........	500
Henry Kendall College, Muskogee, I. T............	500
Williamsburg Institute, Williamsburg, Ky..........	500
Wesleyan University, University Place, Neb........	500
Baylor University, Waco, Tex....................	500
Iowa College, Grinnell, Ia.......................	500
Tulane University of Louisiana, New Orleans, La....	500
State Normal and Industrial College, Greensboro, N. C..	500

Hiram College, Hiram, Ohio...................... $500
Kingfisher College, Kingfisher, O. T............... 500
Academy of the Visitation, Dubuque, Ia............ 500
Williams Industrial College, Little Rock, Ark........ 500
Ewing College, Ewing, Ill....................... 500
Bethany College, Lindsborg, Kan.................. 500
University of Arizona, Tucson, Ariz................ 500
University of New Mexico, Albuquerque, N. M...... 500
The Mississippi Industrial Institute and College,
    Columbus, Miss............................ 500

CHAPTER IX

THE ST. LOUIS CONVENTION

IMMEDIATELY after the election of 1900 I announced that I would not be a candidate in 1904. Having been defeated twice, the second time by a larger majority of the popular vote and of the electoral college than the first time, I thought that it was not wise to be a candidate again until the things I had fought for were so clearly vindicated as to lead the voters of the party to demand my nomination. And having reached the conclusion that I should not be a candidate, I thought it only fair to others who might be candidates to let them know that I would not be in the field.

The result was a contest for supremacy between the radical element of the party and the conservative element. The conservative element had the advantage in that it was able to point to two defeats under my leadership. This advantage was at once seized upon and the conservative leaders promised victory if they were put in control.

Mr. Hearst announced himself as a candidate and received the support of the more radical of the radicals, but did not command the support of all who had supported me. He was especially weak in the South and when the Convention met, the conservatives had a two thirds majority.

Judge Parker, of New York, was the man on whom they had centered, but his delegates were not for the most part instructed. I recognized the difficult position which I occupied and I recognized, too, that those who had fought for me were very much discouraged by the second defeat. I was in a position to know this. After the 1896 election I received as many as 2500 letters a day, all containing promises of support and assurances of victory in 1900.

After 1900 I received very few letters that expressed hope for the future of the Democratic Party. Most of my correspondents were disappointed; they did not see how we could win after the defeats we had suffered.

As the campaign of 1904 approached, I tried through my paper and in my speeches to awaken an interest in the coming campaign and to organize the radical element of the party to resist the encroachments of the conservatives. But it was useless. I did not think it wise to support any particular man for the nomination, and this was probably a mistake, for it is difficult to attack a candidate and have no candidate to suggest in his place. A number of Democrats said to me that if I would only pick out a man, they would support him, but if I would not do so, they must select for themselves. I mentioned a number of candidates as available, Mr. Hearst among others. But no other candidate appeared with any considerable strength except Mr. Hearst. Mr. Wall had Wisconsin, and Mr. Gray had Delaware, and Mr. Cockrell had Missouri, but Mr. Hearst had the only considerable following.

I decided to go to the convention as a delegate, at least I announced my willingness to do so, but even in Nebraska a club had been organized to support Mr. Parker and an effort was made to carry the Convention for him. This effort, however, failed and we carried every county, I think, but one, in the state, and the state convention elected a set of delegates who, to a man, supported my position.

I went to the St. Louis convention from a sense of duty and not because I expected to win any victory there, or even to avoid a humiliating defeat. Remembering that the gold Democrats had left the party and by leaving had lost their influence in the party, I was afraid that if the platform was written by the conservative element it would drive a large part of the radical Democrats out of the party. My purpose, therefore, in going to the convention was to get a platform that would not sacrifice what the party had been fighting for, and would, if possible, secure a candidate who could be voted for by those who had been enthusiastic in my support. I was more successful in the matter of the platform than I had hoped to be.

The first fight in the convention was over the Illinois delegation. Mr. Hearst had a considerable majority in the Illinois state convention, but the organization was against him, and the temporary chairman proceeded to run the convention with the gavel without regard to the wishes of the delegates. A crowd had been brought down from Chicago and stationed near the platform to prevent any interference with the program that had been laid down by those in charge.

While they could not prevent a resolution endorsing Mr. Hearst, they selected a delegation, a majority of which was opposed to him, and the selection was made by the most high-handed methods. The delegates from the several congressional districts made a selection of national delegates, but these were ignored and new names substituted to meet the purpose of those in charge.

When I read in the paper an account of the convention, I telegraphed M. F. Dunlap to meet me at St. Louis and I questioned him in regard to the convention. Believing that an outrage had been perpetrated upon the Democrats of Illinois, and believing that the action of the convention might have a decided influence upon the national convention, I proposed that a contest be made. I went to Chicago and laid the matter before Mr. Hearst, but he felt that it might be a reflection upon the instructions for him to attack the convention that gave the instructions. Mr. Dunlap and I then decided to make the fight ourselves, and each bearing half the expense, we proceeded to secure a petition from a majority of the delegates of the convention asking for the seating of certain men as delegates at large and of the men who had been chosen in the several districts by a majority vote.

WILLIAM JENNINGS BRYAN

Before the convention met we had a signed request of more than a majority of those who actually took part in the convention asking for the action which we suggested. Of course, this was resisted and the Parker men being in control of the convention, the contestants were overruled and the opposing delegates seated. I got a proxy from the Nebraska member of the Committee on Credentials and went into the committee and presented a minority report. I opened and closed the debate on this question and it was the first victory won in the convention, for, although I was voted down by the convention, even without the delegates, I had such an overwhelming majority of the audience with me, that their expression of opinion very much strengthened me in the contest that followed.

The *Post-Dispatch*, one of the Parker papers, had a two-column editorial entitled "The Passing of Bryan," in which the editor discussed at some length the insignificant part that I was taking in the convention. I had entered the convention the day before while some one was speaking and I took my seat unnoticed. This was commented upon as an indication that I no longer had influence in the party.

The delegates had just about had time to read that editorial when I entered the convention to make the minority report; and possibly because of the vindictive spirit that ran through the editorial, my entrance was made the occasion for a demonstration that lasted some twenty minutes. This was the first notice served upon the delegates that they were not to have things all their own way. The reception accorded my speech in behalf of the Illinois contestants increased the impression, and by the time I took up the fight in the full committee, the conservative element was aware that I had with me a large majority of the audience and a respectable minority in the convention.

I was of course a member of the Resolutions Committee, being selected for the place by my own delegation. Senator Daniel was made the chairman of the committee and he appointed a sub-committee to draft the platform. As a matter of courtesy I was put on this sub-committee, but I was the only one in the beginning who represented our side of the fight. Senator Newlands was afterwards added and he was of great assistance in the struggle which followed.

We spent one session, lasting from eight o'clock until midnight, on the tariff plank, and I was finally voted down. During the next session I was occupied in the convention in the fight over the Illinois delegation, and while I was absent the sub-committee went over the rest of the platform and was ready to report to the full committee at the evening session. At the time the committee was appointed the papers published a platform which was described as the platform agreed upon by the leaders of the party. It was not strange that I had not seen the platform, for I was not counted among the leaders by those in control of the convention, and it was not supposed that I would have any influence in the writing of the platform. I had gone over this platform and marked the planks to which I objected and had this copy with me when the full committee met to consider the work of the sub-committee. I took my place at the table not far from Senator Daniel, and we began the most memorable contest through which I have ever passed.

From eight o'clock in the evening until noon the next day—sixteen hours—the battle raged over the wording of that platform. As we took up plank after plank, I moved to strike out and to substitute, and as fortune would have it, I succeeded in securing a majority for each proposition, so that when the platform was completed, I had written a great deal more of it than I had written of the Chicago platform upon which I myself ran. I did not get into the platform all that I wanted, but with the help of a majority of the committee, I kept out of the platform everything to which I objected.

The fight over the gold plank attracted most attention, although the majority against the gold plank was larger than the majority against any other plank stricken out. The vote, as I recall it, was thirty or thirty-five to fifteen. Nearly all of the Southern members voted against this plank. While I voted against it, I did not take much part in the argument, because there were plenty of Parker men to talk against it.

At one time Senator Daniel, who was urging the plank, asked if any Democrat thought that the adoption of the plank would weaken the party in his state. More than half of the committee arose, among them some of Mr. Parker's stanchest supporters.

During the course of the discussion, I asked Senator Hill when he had decided that the gold plank should be inserted in the platform. He replied that he had reached that decision only a few days before the convention. In asking the question I thought that he might answer that he had believed so for months, and I then intended to ask him why it had not been inserted in the New York platform —that platform having been silent upon the subject. His answer, however, showed that it was a newly conceived purpose. I also asked him Judge Parker's views on the subject and he said that he did not know. I asked him if he had ever talked with Judge Parker on the subject and he said that he had not. This seemed remarkable to me and it struck the convention in the same way when the conversation was reported to the convention.

I saw that it was impossible to secure the insertion of any money plank, and I did not, therefore, spend much time in urging it. I consented to a plank suggested by Senator Carmack which stated that the quantitative theory of money had been established and that the increase in the volume of money had removed the money question from the arena of politics. But that plank was objected to by Senator Hill, and seeing that the best we could do was to prevent any expression on the subject, we contented ourselves with leaving out the money question entirely.

THE ST. LOUIS CONVENTION

I urged a plank in favor of the income tax, but while nearly every member of the committee, excepting Senator Hill, expressed himself as favoring the income tax, a considerable majority opposed the insertion of the plank, some of them on the ground that it would interfere with the collection of a campaign fund. I finally agreed to withdraw the income-tax plank if the committee would agree to a stronger anti-trust plank, and when this was consented to, Senator Hill and I drew up an anti-trust plank, it being made as strong as the committee would permit. The labor planks were also inserted during the debate. There were two questions upon which there was no dispute, the election of senators by the people and the party's position on the subject of imperialism. The committee was unanimous on these questions.

The fight over the tariff question was probably the closest and most spirited fight that we had. The original proposition was strongly suggestive of protection, at least it gave very little encouragement to the tariff reformer. Several of the Parker men joined with us in strengthening this plank, among them Mr. Cable, of Illinois, who had been instructed for Mr. Hearst and was in sympathy with the Western element of the party, and Mr. Hamlin, of Massachusetts. Senator Bailey did efficient work on this plank, going so far as to threaten to bring in a minority report if they attempted to report the plank that was suggested in the original draft of the platform. During the course of the discussion I had somewhat spirited debates with several members of the committee, but while the feeling was quite intense on both sides, the debates were conducted with courtesy and no ill feeling was left when the committee adjourned.

I am not sure that I ever rendered my party more service than I did during this fight over the platform, for the platform which we adopted did not surrender the party's position on the questions which had been an issue before, it

151

merely left out some things about which we could not agree. The convention breathed a sigh of relief when the announcement was made that the committee had agreed upon a platform, and the platform was adopted by the unanimous vote of the convention.

As soon as the platform was adopted, the presentation of candidates began, and Judge Parker, Mr. Hearst, and Senator Cockrell were presented. Then came the seconding speeches. As the time rolled on these speeches were limited to four minutes. When Nebraska was called, I arose and yielded to Wisconsin, that Wisconsin might present Mr. Wall. When Wisconsin was called the state yielded to Nebraska and I seconded the nomination of Senator Cockrell.

I was somewhat in a quandary as to what to do.. My main object was to prevent the nomination of Judge Parker, who was so closely identified with the men who had defeated the party in two campaigns that I felt sure he would be so handicapped by this support as to make his election impossible.

I had no particular choice in selecting Senator Cockrell, but was governed by two considerations. First, he stood for everything that I had been fighting for and I could therefore urge his nomination without surrendering or abandoning anything. In the second place, he was an ex-Confederate soldier and I thought that there was a possibility that with him we might break the Southern support of Judge Parker, and I believed that Senator Cockrell would poll a very much larger vote than Judge Parker could possibly poll.

I had more to say than I could say in four minutes, and therefore I asked for a suspension of that rule. I announced to Congressman Clark, the presiding officer, that if allowed unlimited time, I would second the nomination of Senator Cockrell, but if the request was denied I would present the name of someone else for nomination, because in making a nominating speech there was no limit upon time.

Mr. Clark asked the convention for unanimous consent to suspend the rule, and although it was four o'clock in the morning, and the delegates were weary, no objection was made. I have always regarded this as a compliment as well as a great courtesy. Two thirds of the delegates were for Parker and they knew that I was against him; I had fought him and the platform which his leaders had urged, and yet there was no objection when I asked unanimous consent for a suspension as to the time limit, that I might address the convention against Mr. Parker's nomination.

The speech made on that occasion is a matter of record and is generally known as the "I Have Kept the Faith" speech, for what was considered the most striking passage in it was the one in which I stated, in returning the standard which had been placed in my hands, that they could dispute whether I had fought a good fight; they could dispute whether I had finished my course, but they could not deny that I had kept the faith. (See Chapter XXI.)

My effort, however, was futile. The delegates had gone so far in their determination to nominate Judge Parker that no effort of mine could prevent it, and when the roll was called, he had the necessary two thirds. If I had been asked my opinion as to the availability of candidates, I would have decided in favor of Governor Pattison of Pennsylvania. He was the one man suggested who would have been acceptable as a compromise candidate.

Judge Parker was acceptable to the Eastern element, but not to the radical element of the party. Mr. Hearst was acceptable to the radicals, but not to the conservatives. Mr. Gray would have been more acceptable to the conservatives than to the radicals. Mr. Wall, while not for silver in 1896, supported the ticket and would have been acceptable to the radicals, but he lived too far west for the conservatives. Governor Pattison was a candidate before the Chicago convention and was a gold Democrat, but he supported the ticket that year. He lived in the East, but he had a record that commended him to the radicals, and I believed then, and still believe, that he came nearer meeting the requirements of the occasion than any other man we had, but his own delegation sided in with New York and left him no chance.

He died soon after the convention and as his death would have demoralized our campaign, it is fortunate he was not nominated. Notwithstanding the fact that I was looked upon as a disturber of harmony, I had been anxious that we should find some one upon whom the party could unite and for whom we could make a strong fight.

After being up all night for two nights—one night on the Committee on Resolutions and another at the convention (and I had only slept for a few hours for several preceding nights)—I was utterly exhausted and as soon as I concluded my speech, I returned to the hotel and retired. In fact, it was more than fatigue. I went to the convention with a severe cold and it developed so far as to threaten pneumonia. It was against the advice of my physician that I attended the convention, and the first night I attended the meeting of the Committee on Resolutions wearing a mustard plaster over my chest. As soon as I reached the hotel the doctor put a plaster of antiphlogistine on my chest and I remained in bed until night. During the day Judge Parker sent his famous telegram which threw the convention into an uproar. The delegates brought me news from time to time and no one could foresee the result. Several delegates came over and expressed themselves in very emphatic language to the effect that they "had been bunkoed." I tried to soothe them by telling them that it was no more than they might have expected and that they ought to have known from the tactics pursued that it was not a compromise which had been demanded but a surrender.

Finally the situation became so tense that I decided to

go over to the convention. Taking advantage of the absence of the physician, I dressed and hurried over, pale and worn. I went to the platform and made my last stand against the Parker element. His telegram had announced that he regarded the gold standard as irrevocably established and the Resolutions Committee brought in a resolution declaring that as the question was no longer an issue, his personal opinion was not material. I introduced an amendment calling upon him to give his opinion upon certain other phases of the money question, as he had seen fit to give it upon the gold question. But after reflection I withdrew this, not only because there was little chance of its adoption, but because I was afraid that his answers to my questions, if he answered them, would simply commit him to the wrong side of the question.

When the vote was taken the committee's resolution was adopted by about the same vote which was cast in favor of his nomination, and the resolution was not a very important one after all, because it only stated the fact which we all recognized, namely, that the money question was not an issue any longer. It would have been better, however, if the resolution had stated that it was no longer an issue because the principle contended for by the Democrats had been vindicated and because an unexpected increase of money from another source had rendered the restoration of bimetallism unnecessary.

His telegram, however, put an end to whatever hope there was of Mr. Parker's election. He had remained silent and by so doing he had alienated the rank and file of the party. If the election had occurred a week after the convention, he would scarcely have received half the votes of the party, but as time went on, the Democrats became more reconciled to the situation and recognized that he had simply expressed his own opinion and in no wise committed the party.

I took part in the campaign, justifying myself by the

fact that the Democratic platform was good as far as it went and that our candidate stood for a number of reforms, while President Roosevelt was pledged to no reforms. I offered my services to the national committee and spoke in several of the states, neglecting my own state to do so. And while I have reason to believe that I was instrumental in increasing his vote, I found it difficult to arouse enthusiasm.

I heard many amusing stories of the campaign illustrating the lack of enthusiasm. One man told me that at a ratification meeting three cheers were proposed. The chairman gave two of them and the man who told me gave one, which made the three—the remainder of the audience refused to join. At a meeting in Indiana where the Democratic candidate for governor was present, the chairman proposed three cheers for the ticket and got no response whatever, but the audience, after giving three cheers for the Republican candidate, adjourned.

I look back to the St. Louis convention as one of the best illustrations I have had of the fact that one cannot see very far ahead. I went to the convention expecting to be disregarded by a hostile majority. I never knew one hour what was coming next, but continued on my way meeting the questions as they arose and doing what seemed to me to be right at the time.

In the convention in which I expected humiliation I found victory, for I think the victory at St. Louis was really a greater personal triumph than the victory at Chicago, and did more to strengthen me in the party. My support of the ticket convinced many who had doubted my democracy that I was in fact democratic in my principles and loyal to the Democratic party as an organization.

When I went to St. Louis I could not, of course, see the outcome, and I would not promise in advance to support the nominee, but I was convinced during the course of the convention that the Democratic party was sound at heart and that its surrender to the conservative element was but temporary.

This encouraged me to continue the fight within the Democratic party, and the platform was such that I had something to stand on and to fight for. The platform committed our candidate to certain important reforms, while the Republican platform committed the President to no specific reforms, and I felt that if we could but get rid of imperialism and the spirit of war which the President seemed to embody, we might be better prepared to enter upon the fight for economic reforms.

Looking back upon the campaign of 1904, I think that it was probably best that Mr. Parker was nominated, because his nomination gave the conservatives a chance to test their ability to win victory, and their failure made it possible for the party to reorganize itself and become a positive and progressive force. Had we nominated a radical at that time, he would, in all probability, have been defeated, because the conservative element would not have supported him; had we nominated a compromise candidate he would also, in all probability, have been defeated, but the nomination of a man clearly identified with the Wall Street element removed, for the present at least, the fear of another conservative triumph in the party.

At the Democratic National Convention at Denver in 1908 Mr. Bryan was nominated for President for the third time. His position on the Trust question at that time is set forth in a statement and telegrams which will be found in the Appendix.

CHAPTER X

The Baltimore Convention

AFTER my third defeat in 1908 I felt that nothing but a revolutionary change in the political situation would justify a fourth nomination. Not seeing evidence of such a change and not being willing to obstruct the plans of other aspirants, I announced that I would not be a candidate in 1912. As a result of the Congressional election in 1910 the Democrats gained control of the House of Representatives and Champ Clark was elected Speaker.

Clark entered Congress in 1892, from which time my acquaintance with him began. As is the custom, he came to Washington after his election and before his term began in March of 1893. I recall our first meeting at that time. He said that he had used my record as an argument in his race for the nomination. The Democratic member of Congress from his district was serving his first term when Clark announced his candidacy. His argument against the sitting member was that he had not accomplished anything during his first term. The member replied that it was not customary for a new member to do much during his first term; that it took time for a man to secure prominence and influence in Congress. I had been made a member of the Ways and Means Committee during my first term when I was only a little past thirty.

From that time on I met Clark in the 53d Congress and afterwards at Democratic national gatherings. While I was not more intimate with him than I was with a thousand other Democrats scattered throughout the Union, I followed his record with interest and rejoiced at his growing influence.

After his election to the Speakership in 1911 I regarded him as the logical candidate and invited him to speak at my

158

birthday banquet on March 19, 1911. My purpose in inviting him was to let those who were friendly to me know that I regarded him as an available man for the nomination. Governor Wilson was being talked of more and more, but I felt that Clark was more in sympathy with the policies of the party and, therefore, better suited to lead our forces in the coming presidential campaign. Clark came, but I learned from him afterwards that it was with some reluctance. This surprised me and I was surprised still more when, as the campaign proceeded, I found that his friends were tying up with the Harmon forces wherever a combination was necessary to defeat the Wilson forces.

Wilson, on the other hand, was becoming more radical in his utterances and was gathering about him an increasing number of the progressive element of the party. He was also exciting the opposition of the reactionary element. As the campaign proceeded I received many letters from different parts of the country warning me that Harmon men were getting on Clark delegations.

Having learned from a friend who was present at the meeting that Wall Street had picked out Governor Harmon as its Democratic candidate, I at once brought the matter to the attention of the Democrats of the country and insisted that he could not expect to be the candidate of a progressive Democratic Party. I was fond of Harmon personally, but I was satisfied that his business connections and his bias made it impossible for him to be the exponent of the masses in their struggle for reforms. I had confidence in Clark personally, and, knowing that a man cannot refuse the support of those who for different reasons may favor him, continued to count Clark and Wilson as equally acceptable to the progressive element of the party.

In the Nebraska primary I announced myself as a candidate for delegate-at-large, saying that I would willingly support either Clark or Wilson according to instructions, but that I would resign as delegate in case the state

159

instructed for Harmon, giving as a reason that I was not willing to aid in turning the party over to Wall Street. I ran about five thousand ahead of the ticket and considered my election as an endorsement of my opposition to Wall Street domination.

Some of my prominent political friends came into Nebraska and made an active canvass of the state in favor of Clark and against Wilson. George Fred Williams and Ex-Senator Pettigrew were among the number. They were both strongly against Wilson. They quoted Adrian Joline's letter and also extracts from Mr. Wilson's utterances on the money question. They urged the support of Clark on the ground that he always supported the things that I advocated and was, therefore, nearer to me in his political ideas and ideals. I favored a division of the delegation so as to avoid a fight between two progressive candidates, but Mr. Wilson's manager insisted on having two thirds of the delegation and thus prevented a joint ticket.

I was so anxious to preserve an attitude of perfect neutrality between the two that I tried to make the vote in my precinct as nearly equal as possible. There were two voters at my home and I advised them to vote one for Clark and one for Wilson. Had they done so there would have been only one vote difference between the votes of the candidates, but when the time approached they thought that one of the candidates was going to have quite a lead and so, following the spirit instead of the letter of my advice, voted together for the one they thought was weakest, but were mistaken in their calculations and their two votes thus gave the successful candidate a lead of three majority over the other.

When the returns from the state came in it was found that Clark had the instructions but that Wilson had a majority of the delegates (bound by instructions, of course, but friendly to Wilson).

Some time in the spring, Norman E. Mack, the committeeman from New York, wrote me and asked if I would like to be temporary chairman. I answered that I did not think it would be wise for me to be temporary chairman. My reason for not wanting to enter the race was that some of the metropolitan papers were construing my neutrality between the two leading candidates as evidence of a desire to be a candidate myself. I was afraid that I would be accused of trying to stampede the convention, that being the possibility upon which the unfriendly papers dwelt at greatest length.

As the convention approached it became apparent that the progressives would be in control of the convention and that Clark would have more votes, although neither would have a majority.

I wrote to Governor Wilson and suggested to him that we should have a progressive chairman and that as neither had a majority the choice would naturally fall to the candidate having the largest number of votes. I called his attention to the fact that Ollie James, the candidate of the Clark delegates, was a progressive and a fair-minded man and suggested that he accept James in case it should prove impossible to elect the man of his own choice. He answered, saying that he preferred O'Gorman. I mention this fact to combat the unfair criticism of Mr. Clark's friends directed against me after I changed my vote.

At Chicago I watched the Republican Convention select a candidate under the pressure of influence from Wall Street. What I saw there made me sensitive to the influence of Wall Street in our own convention. While I was at Chicago the Democratic National Committee met and selected Judge Parker as temporary chairman. In the contest before the committee the Clark men had supported Ollie James and the Wilson men Judge O'Gorman. Neither having a majority, Parker finally received the support of the Clark men and became the choice of the committee. Josephus Daniels, then the member of the committee for North

Part of Mr. Bryan's copy of his letter to Champ Clark

THE BALTIMORE CONVENTION

Ft. Wayne, Ind.

May 30

My dear Clark:—

I venture to make a suggestion for your consideration. I believe the fight over wool will prove a crisis in your life as well as in the party's prospects. A leader must *lead;* it is not always pleasant to oppose friends, and one who leads takes the chances of defeat, but these are the necessary attendants upon leadership. Wilson is making friends because he *fights.* His fight against Smith was heroic. He fought for the income tax and for a primary law. The people like a fighter. You won your position by fighting and you must continue to fight to hold it. Enter into the wool fight. Don't be content to take polls and sit in the background. Take one side or the other and take it *strong.* If a tax on wool is right, lead the protectionists to victory. You can do it and it will make you strong with that wing of the party. If free wool is right, as I believe it is, lead the fight for it and get the credit for the victory if victory comes. Don't inquire about how the fight is going to go—make it go the right way if you can. If you fail you lay the foundation for a future victory. The right wins in the end—don't be afraid to wait. My opinion is that you will not have to wait long, but whether long or not, one can better afford to be defeated fighting for the right than to win on the wrong side. I hope you will pardon this intrusion upon your thoughts, but the party needs your assistance—a blast from your bugle may save the day, and it will, in my judgment, strengthen you personally.

Regards to the family.

Yours

Bryan

163

Carolina, called me up by telephone and asked me what I thought of the selection. I told him that I not only would criticise the selection but the committee that made the selection. I then prepared a telegram to each progressive candidate reading as follows:

"In the interest of harmony I suggested to the sub-committee of the Democratic National Committee the advisability of recommending as temporary chairman some progressive acceptable to the leading progressive candidates for the presidential nomination. I took it for granted that no committeeman interested in Democratic success would desire to offend the members of a convention overwhelmingly progressive by naming a reactionary to sound the keynote of the campaign. Eight members of the sub-committee, however, have, over the protest of the remaining eight, agreed upon not only a reactionary, but upon the one Democrat, who, among those not candidates for the presidential nomination is, in the eyes of the public, most conspicuously identified with the reactionary element of the party. I shall be pleased to join you and your friends in opposing this selection by the full committee or by the convention. Kindly answer here."

Governor Foss of Massachusetts, Governor Marshall of Indiana, and Governor Baldwin of Connecticut, all declined to join me in my fight against Parker. Governor Wilson of New Jersey and Governor Burke of North Dakota went to my support.

Woodrow Wilson sent the following reply:

"You are right. Before hearing of your message I clearly stated my position in answer to a question from the Baltimore *Evening Sun*. The Baltimore convention is to be the convention of progressives—the men who are progressive in principle and by conviction. It must, if it is not to be put in a wrong light before the country, express its convictions in its organization and its choice of the men who are to speak for it. You are to be a member of the convention and are entirely within your rights in doing everything within your power to oring that result about. No one will doubt where my sympathies lie, and you will, I am sure, find my friends in the convention acting upon a clear conviction and always in the interest of the people's cause. I am happy in the confidence that they need no suggestion from me."

Champ Clark replied as follows:

"Have consulted with committee having my interests in charge and agree with them that the supreme consideration should be to prevent any discord in the convention. Friends of mine on the sub-committee of arrangements have already presented the name of Ollie James to the sub-committee. I believe that if all join in the interest of harmony in an appeal to the entire national committee to avoid controversies in matters of organization that the committee will so arrange as to leave the platform and nomination of candidates as the only real issues on which delegates need divide."

Governor Marshall's reply was:

"You may be right, but as Judge Parker, as a member of the committee on resolutions from the state of New York at the national convention at Denver, helped to report our platform of 1908 and as he came to Indiana that year to advocate your election and mine, and as he returned in 1910 to advocate the election of Senator Kern, I do not see how his selection as temporary chairman will result in a reactionary platform in 1912."

Governor Burke of North Dakota sent the only explicit acceptance of the challenge offered by the Wall Street crowd. Governor Marshall was willing to support Parker, while Clark's answer was a straddle. Governor Wilson's telegram, while not as direct as I would have liked, began with a sentence that led the delegates to accept it as a promise to oppose the Parker candidacy, which his delegates did. The account of this incident is given by Governor Wilson's secretary, J. P. Tumulty, in his book on "Wilson as I Knew Him," page 105.

I soon afterwards left the Chicago Convention and proceeded to Baltimore, hoping all the way that the Clark delegates would oppose Parker and thus give us a progressive temporary chairman to sound the keynote of the convention. When I reached Baltimore I found the situation unchanged. A Clark delegate called on me soon after my arrival and intimated that I might have the permanent chairmanship if I did not oppose Parker. Of course, I did not entertain any such proposition, but proceeded to hunt for a candidate to put up against Parker, after having made a personal appeal to Parker himself. I had a frank talk with him on the afternoon before the convention met in which I told him that he had no part in the reforms for which the party now stood and could not possibly give expression to the thoughts and purposes of the delegates who constituted a majority of a progressive convention. I made no impression on him further than to arouse his ire, as such a protest naturally would.

I first called in Ollie James, the candidate of the Clark men when the matter was before the committee. I felt sure that he could defeat Parker. He laid the matter before Mr. Clark's managers and returned to tell me that they objected to it and that therefore he could not allow his name to be used as a candidate. I then sent for Judge O'Gorman, Mr. Wilson's candidate in the contest, but he, being a member of the New York delegation, had pledged his support to Judge Parker, although he advised Judge Parker not to be a candidate.

Failing to secure a candidate from the delegates supporting Clark and Wilson, I made an appeal to Senator Kern, but found that he, too, was embarrassed by the fact that he was there as delegate supporting Governor Marshall. The Indiana delegates, following the wishes of Governor Marshall, were nearly all supporting Judge Parker. The matter was made more delicate for Senator Kern by the fact that he was already being discussed as a candidate and naturally hesitated to do anything that would divert attention from his state's candidate to himself. Senator Kern urged me to be a candidate for the place as others had, but I explained to him that my first desire was to present an argument against Judge Parker's candidacy, which I could not do if I was myself a candidate for the place.

When Senator Kern left my room the night before the opening of the Convention he did not answer positively whether he would allow me to present his name, but said he hoped I would not. I heard next morning, not from him directly but indirectly, that he had a plan, but I did not learn the details of it. Not having received from Senator Kern a positive refusal to allow his name to be presented, I placed him in nomination after the committee had offered the name of Judge Parker. My speech will be found in the Appendix.

I have regarded my use of the "pillar and cloud" of fire of the children of Israel as one of the most appropriate references that I have ever made to the Bible in a political argument, but there was so much confusion in the convention that it seemed to make but little impression and I think I saw but one reference to it in the papers. It illustrates an experience that one frequently has; a phrase upon which one sets great store is often ignored, while a sentence which is spoken on the spur of the moment and without thought of its being considered important, will attract widespread attention.

WILLIAM JENNINGS BRYAN

In the course of my speech against Parker I used a quotation from Tennyson, "He never sold the truth to serve the hour," which was printed in large letters over Jefferson's picture which hung at the right of the platform. When I used this quotation Mrs. Bryan, who was just back of the platform, heard a man near her say to another, "I told them that he would use that quotation if they put it up there."

As I look back upon the convention I have a growing appreciation of the part played by Senator Kern; it was the best piece of acting that I ever saw off the stage. In fact, I have not seen it surpassed on the stage. As soon as I had finished my speech he arose and made an appeal to Judge Parker to join him in withdrawing from the contest, that the convention might agree upon some one who could receive the united support of the convention. He made an eloquent plea for harmony and then paused for Judge Parker to answer. There was deathlike silence for a moment. Then Senator Kern appealed to Mr. Murphy, chairman of the New York delegation, to use his influence with Judge Parker to secure his withdrawal in the interest of harmony. Again a silence that was deathlike. Then Senator Kern turned to the presiding officer and in a spirit of defiance announced that if there must be a contest Mr. Bryan was the only man to lead the people's side and placed my name in nomination.

As the roll call proceeded it became apparent that Judge Parker had the support of Governor Harmon's delegates, Congressman Underwood's delegates and a considerable percentage, though not all, of Speaker Clark's delegates. (The vote stood Parker 579, Bryan 508.) Parker was elected, but the victory did not arouse the enthusiasm which might have been expected. The shadow of the vote darkened the convention, because the friends of Mr. Clark began to suspect what its effect would be on the country.

Judge Parker was conducted to the platform to deliver

his address as temporary chairman, but the hall was in confusion and the aisles were full of people going out. So large a percentage of the audience retired that those in charge of the convention hastily conferred and announced that Judge Parker would deliver his address at the evening session and then adjourned the convention. I have not consulted the precedents, but do not know of any similar experience. As soon as it was evident that I was defeated I went with my wife and children to the hotel. They were naturally disappointed and sympathetic, but I explained to them why I had made the fight and assured them that my purpose had been accomplished. I was satisfied that the country would be aroused when it knew that a supposedly progressive convention had selected as temporary chairman the man most conspicuously identified with the Wall Street side.

I was not disappointed. I had scarcely reached the hotel before telegrams of congratulation began to pour in. Then followed such a demonstration of the power of public opinion as has never been witnessed in a convention before or since. The effect of the contest upon the Democrats of the country was electrical. The party, sound at heart, felt that it was being betrayed by its political leaders and "the folks at home" communicated with the delegates. Many joined in one telegram, the language varying from courteous appeal to vehement denunciation.

The Montana delegation was cast for me with the exception of one vote. The result was immediately carried by bulletins throughout the country and shortly the Montana delegation received a brief telegram signed by a number of angry citizens saying, in substance, "Send us the name of the —— who voted for Parker. We want to meet him when he comes home."

These telegrams continued to pour in during the convention as each new incident gave new excuse for expression. The total number of telegrams received, according to the local agents of the two telegraph companies, was estimated at one hundred and ten thousand, or an average of about one hundred to a delegate. I received 1182 telegrams and they averaged three names to a telegram. One of them, from Virginia, was signed by one hundred and forty names. I learned later as I traveled through the West that the Democrats in the agricultural section would congregate at the railroad stations, read the bulletins as they were taken from the wire, and then join in sending a telegram to the delegates whom they knew, the signers "chipping in," as they say, to pay the expense of the telegrams.

When I was given credit for having exerted an influence on the convention, I replied that I had simply turned the faucet and allowed public sentiment to flow in upon the convention, deserving no personal credit except for knowing where the faucet was and the height of the stand-pipe from which the public opinion flowed.

But to return to my narrative; early in the evening a committee from Mr. Clark's headquarters called to offer me the permanent chairmanship of the convention. This encouraged my family and the friends about headquarters, because it was proof conclusive that Mr. Clark's managers were feeling the reaction from the victory of the afternoon. I declined the invitation, telling the messengers that those who owned a ship should furnish the crew; that when my friends controlled a convention, we never asked the minority to supply the officers. We were all kept up late that night listening to the messages that came from the various headquarters, all indicating confusion and consternation.

The next morning I was delayed in getting to the Committee on Resolutions and found when I reached the convention hall that a committee had been sent to the hotel in my absence to ask me to accept the chairmanship of the Committee on Resolutions. They soon returned and made me the offer. I expressed my appreciation of the honor done me, but suggested that the majority should furnish

170

the chairman, as it might become necessary for me to present a minority report and it would not look well for such a report to be presented by the chairman. Mr. Kern was then chosen chairman and I was asked if I would serve on the sub-committee. This I gladly consented to do, as I desired to contribute as much as possible to the making of a progressive platform.

Before the sub-committee withdrew to begin its work I offered a resolution to the effect that the committee after agreeing upon a platform should hold it until after the nomination of a candidate for President, so that he might be consulted about the platform before it was adopted. One of the Eastern delegates arose and asked in a tone of surprise whether I thought it possible that a nominee of the convention would object to any platform that the convention had adopted. I replied, "Our candidate did in 1904." The questioner subsided amid the laughter of the committee, and the resolution was adopted.

We then had an illustration of the sensational character of reports that are sent out from conventions. The morning papers under big headlines told about my being defeated for chairman, the unfriendly papers in varying tones of gleefulness described my demise. The afternoon papers with headlines as large announced that Mr. Bryan had risen from the grave and taken charge of the Committee on Resolutions—basing the statement on the fact that the innocent resolution that I had introduced had been adopted.

My association with the other members of the sub-committee was pleasant and harmonious. I never worked with a more congenial crowd. The completeness of the harmony may be gathered from an incident. Just before the opening of the second day's session I met Judge O'Gorman, who told me that Senator Martin had stated to him that instead of being a firebrand as some of the committee feared I would be, I was the most conservative man on the committee. When the committee assembled I went up to

171

Senator Martin and addressing him in serious tones said, "Senator, I am sorry to hear you have been making unkind remarks about me."

The Senator assured me, with a look of honest surprise upon his face, that I had been misinformed, that he had spoken of me only in the most kind and complimentary language.

"But," I explained to him, "you told Judge O'Gorman that I was the most conservative man on this committee. What will my friends think when they hear this and know that you are on the committee?"

He enjoyed the humor of it and we went on working together as if we had always agreed on the policies of the party.

I assured the committee that I had no desire to write into the platform of another candidate any view that I had that had not already been endorsed by the party. I opposed any retreat on public questions and found the committee quite ready to endorse all that the Democrats in Congress had done since they believed, as I did, that our fight must be made upon the party's record. I was successful in reiterating in our platform many of the planks contained in previous platforms which I had helped to write, but I did not ask for the incorporation of anything new. The platform incorporated a phrase which had appeared in three previous platforms, namely, "A private monopoly is indefensible and intolerable." I first used the phrase in a speech at an Anti-Trust Conference at Chicago in 1899. The sentence used was almost identical with the sentence above quoted, and incorporated in the platform of 1900 and 1904 and 1908 and finally in 1912. I digress far enough from the narrative to say that this sentence was incorporated in President Wilson's speech of acceptance and in his message to Congress on the trust question.

I think I should mention a fact that one plank in the platform which has often been attributed to me, namely the plank reading: "We favor a single Presidential term and to that end urge the adoption of an amendment to the Constitution making the President ineligible for reëlection, and we pledge the candidate of this convention to this principle," was proposed by Governor Beckham of Kentucky. I very gladly supported the plank, but for obvious reasons would like to have it known that I did not offer it at this time. I have always believed in the single term for the President. When in Congress I introduced a resolution, proposing the necessary amendment to the Constitution. In each of my Presidential campaigns I made the statement that if elected I would not be a candidate for a second term, giving my reasons.

I will add that in every speech that I made during the campaign following I pointed out that this pledge against a second term enabled the President to serve the people with singleness of purpose unembarrassed by any selfish interest.

The platform also laid the foundation for the currency legislation secured in President Wilson's first term. The language employed in the discussion of banks was a distinct departure from the language usually employed, just as the language employed in the discussion of labor marked a new departure. The plank on independence to the Philippines was substantially the same as that contained in the three previous platforms of our party. An amendment providing for election of United States Senators by the people advocated in three preceding platforms was urged upon the states.

While I was occupied with the work of the Resolutions Committee most of the time Wednesday and Thursday I was from time to time in conference with the progressive element of the convention and learned of the activity of the same element that had controlled the Republican Convention at Chicago. I found that the representatives of Morgan, Belmont, and Ryan were at work. Belmont and Ryan were themselves delegates, the former from Chicago and the latter from Virginia. Being convinced of the intimate relationship between these financiers and Mr. Murphy, I became increasingly alarmed lest they should be able by the control of the New York delegation to make the nomination. The ninety delegates from New York were bound by the unit rule and Charles P. Murphy, the Tammany leader, had enough delegates to enable him to vote the entire delegation at his will.

When I returned to headquarters Wednesday night my brother, Charles W. Bryan, who had been closely associated with me in Nebraska, laid before me the information he had secured and suggested the resolution which I introduced the next night.

I took Wednesday night to think over the subject, and Thursday morning, before going to the committee room, dictated a resolution along the line he had suggested and left instructions that he call in as many of our friends as possible and get their opinion on it. The resolution, as I had prepared it, contained two paragraphs; the first was substantially the resolution as adopted by the convention; the second embodied the plan that was the outgrowth of my own experience in my three campaigns.

> "*Resolved*, That in this crisis in our party's career and in our country's history this convention sends greetings to the people of the United States, and assures them that the party of Jefferson and of Jackson is still the champion of popular government and equality before the law. As proof of our fidelity to the people, we hereby declare ourselves opposed to the nomination of any candidate for President who is the representative of or under obligation to J. Pierpont Morgan, Thomas F. Ryan, August Belmont, or any other member of the privilege-hunting and favor-seeking class.
>
> "*Be It Further Resolved*, That we demand the with-

174

drawal from this convention of any delegate or delegates constituting or representing the above-named interests."

I had never had a national committee entirely loyal. In the first campaign some of my committee did not attend the meetings. They were opposed to my election and yet retained their membership on the committee. The situation was so bad in 1900 that I thought that the committeemen who represented predatory wealth had little sense of political honor and should not remain on the committee when they were not in sympathy with the aims of the party. In the second paragraph, therefore, I included authority for the removal of unfriendly members of the committee.

When I returned to the hotel Thursday evening I found my brother very much discouraged, as he said that none of the men whom he consulted thought it wise to introduce the resolution, the criticism being directed mainly to the second paragraph which they thought might arouse opposition on the ground that it interfered with the rights of the states to select committeemen.

All my political friends appeared to be at the hall at the time and I suggested that I might strike out the second paragraph, whereupon he expressed a fear that the first paragraph alone might not draw the line with sufficient clearness.

He suggested a second sentence that dealt with Belmont and Ryan, who were delegates, in order to put teeth in it as he said. I framed the sentence, embodying his suggestion, and started for the convention not quite certain whether to chance the resolution or not. On the way to the convention I decided to introduce it. I felt some timidity about taking the responsibility without any encouragement from those who were nearest to me and most in sympathy with what I was trying to do, and reached the decision more from conviction that it was

175

my duty to act than from reasons with which I could justify the act.

As I went to the platform some one pulled me aside to introduce me to Mrs. Taft. This little incident led me to change a sentence in the first paragraph referring to Mr. Taft's nomination in Chicago. I had included a few words not necessary to the resolution but comparing the attempt that was being made in our convention with the successful effort of Wall Street to control the Chicago nomination. When I found that Mrs. Taft was there I felt that it would be ungenerous to give her pain by such a reference to her husband and I therefore struck out the offensive words. President Taft afterwards learned of it, and in his characteristic way thanked me for the consideration shown his wife.

I do not recall just who took part in the debate on the Morgan-Belmont-Ryan resolution. Flood of Virginia led off with a denunciation of the resolution. He stood at one side of me a few feet away. I next met him after I became Secretary of State. He was chairman of the Foreign Relations Committee of the House and called at the Department on some matter in connection with his committee. I did not recognize him until he gave me his name and then I made him feel at home by remarking, "The last time I saw you I saw only your profile."

Honorable Cone Johnson of Texas made a speech in which he condensed a great deal in a few words. I became better acquainted with him afterwards when he came into the State Department as solicitor.

I went to Permanent Chairman Ollie James and asked for his recognition. It was necessary to suspend the rules and that required a two-thirds vote. I have many reasons to cherish the friendship of Ollie James, but he never did me a greater favor than when he recognized me on this occasion.

The resolution came as a surprise to my friends as well as to our opponents. "Dropping a bombshell into the

crowd" is a phrase often used to describe the sudden pre-
cipitation of an issue. The phrase never more accurately
described a situation. The explosion was immediate and
vehement. The convention was in an uproar. Many were
on their feet shouting denunciation. Old politicians accus-
tomed to surprises in conventions were dazed. One member
of the Congress rushed to the platform and, gesticulating
violently, denounced me until he frothed at the mouth,
and almost hysterical he was carried away by friends. I
sat upon the platform where I could see the seething crowd.
Urey Woodson, near me, was one of the Parker crowd. He
was my friend in the earlier campaigns, but went off with
Wall Street element in 1904 and had become prominent
among the reactionaries. His apostasy had not led to any
rupture in our relationship, although we understood that
we were no longer co-workers. He had a box near me and
was watching the proceedings as much mystified as his
associates on the floor of the convention. I was near enough
to him to remark, calling him by his first name, "When
your machine ran over me it moved so slowly that I was
able to inspect the works from the underside and I am now
telling the convention what I saw."

My aim was to get a roll call, because I felt that whichever way the convention voted it would be difficult to
nominate a man who had the support of the New York
delegation. If they passed the resolution it excluded anyone who was the representative of Morgan, Belmont, or
Ryan or under their influence; if they voted it down, the
rebuke from the country would make it impossible for New
York to select a candidate.

Just before the roll was called I announced that I would
strike out the second paragraph of the resolution. I do
not know how many in the convention understood what
I had done; they were too excited to distinguish between
the two paragraphs. When the roll was called the tumult
reached its height. A state would be called; its chairman

would announce its full vote, "aye." Then half the delegation would jump to their feet and demand a poll, shaking their fists and shouting in violent language. I do not think there were ever before so many people in one hall, wildly excited and swearing at one another without someone being hurt. I heard afterwards of delegates who were loudly expressing the hope that somebody would take me out and hang me. One delegate, whom I afterward aided to a high position, stated that he would give twenty-five thousand dollars to anybody who would kill me. I have no thought that these men who poured out their threats would have carried them out. I only mention them to show the state of super-excitement.

Polls were taken in nearly all the delegations and some of them changed from a solid vote against the resolution to a solid vote in favor of it. As the roll call proceeded the opposition became frantic and delegates piled over each other to vote for the resolution, with the result that it finally carried by a vote of about $4\frac{1}{2}$ to 1. Even New York voted for the resolution.

Some one reported to me afterwards that Murphy turned to Belmont and said, "August, listen and hear yourself vote yourself out of the convention." Virginia voted $23\frac{1}{2}$ votes for the resolution. It was a great victory for progressive Democracy. Nearly all the Wilson delegates voted for the resolution and nearly all of the Clark delegates also, although many of the Clark leaders voted "no" and in so doing greatly lessened the political chances of their candidate. Clark's leaders are more responsible for his defeat than Clark himself, or would have been if it were possible for a candidate for President to excuse himself for allowing his managers to do what he would not do himself.

The effect of the Morgan-Belmont-Ryan resolution can hardly be overestimated. One of the London papers compared it with St. George slaying the dragon. One of the Baltimore papers pictured it in a cartoon as burning the word "progressive" into the hide of the Democratic donkey. The passage of the resolution stirred the enthusiasm of the progressive Democrats and gave a new impetus to the shower of telegrams from the rank and file of the party. Having, as I thought, insured the convention against the nomination of anyone by Wall Street influence, I retired from the convention, while the delegates proceeded to place candidates in nomination.

Balloting began on Friday. Up to this time I had not taken my seat with my delegation, although I had appeared twice on the platform—Tuesday, when I made my speech against Parker, and Thursday night, when I introduced the Morgan-Belmont-Ryan resolution. My reason for absenting myself was that I did not want to risk attracting attention, having in mind the oft-repeated charge of unfriendly papers that I wanted to stampede the convention in my own favor. My intention was to keep out of the hall until the nomination was made and then appear at a time when I could make a speech in support of the candidate, whoever he might be.

On Friday night I was in the room of the Resolutions Committee when a great demonstration broke out in the convention hall. After waiting a while for it to subside, I went to the hall to inquire the cause. I found the convention in an uproar—the New York delegation had gone over to Clark on the fifth ballot. New York had started out voting for Harmon, thus verifying my predictions in regard to Wall Street's choice. I knew that New York's second choice was Underwood, but the throwing of the vote to Clark was by many believed to be evidence of an understanding between the Clark leaders and the New York delegation. I never heard anything other than circumstantial evidence to support this charge and never made it myself.

I am quite sure that Mr. Clark's leaders had calculated on using the New York delegation to give him a majority vote in the convention and that they then expected to claim his nomination on the ground that he had a majority. One of his leaders had asked me while I was at the Chicago Convention whether I thought any candidate receiving a majority could be prevented from securing two thirds. I answered that I thought there was only one instance when the two thirds rule had ever prevented a majority candidate from receiving the nomination.

I expected the nomination of a majority candidate, not only because precedent favored it but I had never taken kindly to the two thirds rule. I believe that the rule should be changed so as to allow a majority to nominate, and have advocated the change, but I have coupled with it the abolishment of the unit rule, which gives the big states an unfair advantage in the convention. New York, for instance, with a delegation of ninety, can, under the unit rule, exercise a tremendous influence and do so in spite of the protests of nearly half the delegation. If those in control have forty-six delegates of the ninety with them, they can use the other forty-four to carry out their purposes in spite of any protest that the forty-four can make. It was because the New York delegation, under the control of Mr. Murphy, was used to give Mr. Clark a majority delegation that I was not willing to help to swell the vote to two thirds. I felt that during the campaign the party would be unable to deny that Wall Street had exercised a deciding influence in the naming of our candidate. I then entered the fight to prevent not Mr. Clark's nomination only but the nomination of any person by the New York delegation.

While the demonstration was still in progress I took my seat with the Nebraska delegation and from that time until the convention adjourned never left the hall during the sessions of the convention. One of the assistants of the sergeant at arms who was stationed in our part of the hall supplied me with water, keeping a large bottle under the platform, while my brother supplied me with sandwiches. My one thought was to save the Democratic Party from defeat at the polls. I believed then, and have believed ever since, that if the nomination of our candidate was brought about in such a way that the country would regard it as a triumph for Wall Street, he would be defeated no matter who he was.

Ex-President Roosevelt, defeated at Chicago, had not yet decided whether he would enter the field. I felt sure that he would become a candidate if he could charge that Wall Street had nominated both candidates and make his appeal to the progressives of both parties and I felt sure that in such a campaign he would have been successful. I think the result proved this to be true. Mr. Roosevelt took from the Republican Party more than half its vote, polling 4,119,582 votes as against 3,485,082 votes for Mr. Taft. Mr. Taft carried but two states in the electoral college, Utah and Vermont.

As the Democratic Party was more progressive than the Republican Party, what chances would we have had to win with any candidate not free from Wall Street domination? He would have been defeated if he had had to carry in the campaign the handicap of having secured his nomination by the aid of the New York delegation dominated by one man, Charles Murphy, who had back of him the influence of the financiers of Wall Street.

My interest was not in any candidate, but in the party. I was under no personal obligation to either of the candidates. Neither one had exerted himself in my behalf in the primary at which I was chosen delegate. Mr. Wilson had never supported me in my campaigns and Mr. Clark's support, while always given to me, was given to me as thousands of Democrats give their support. Being a candidate for Congress in each of my campaigns, he could not have opposed me without injury to himself, even if he had desired to do so. While, of course, his support was not perfunctory, because he believed in the things for which I stood, still it was never given to me at a sacrifice, and I had done fully as much for him as he ever had done for me. But I digress.

The vote of our delegation was cast solidly for Clark for thirteen ballots. A number of our delegates wanted to leave him as soon as New York went to his support, but I insisted that we should continue to support him, as I expected that New York would throw its vote to Underwood and thus leave Clark to secure his nomination—if he secured it—from the progressive delegates of the convention.

I felt sure from what I had heard that New York really preferred Underwood and would leave Clark at any time its influence could aid Underwood. After the thirteenth ballot the convention adjourned until Saturday morning. Realizing that to keep the promise I had made to the Nebraska Democracy when a candidate for delegate, namely, that I would have no part in turning over the party to Wall Street, and realizing that to carry out this promise it might become necessary to change from Clark* at any moment, I prepared a written statement to be read to the convention when I changed my vote, hoping all the time that it would not be necessary.

This statement was prepared before the convention opened on Saturday morning. I had kept it in my pocket ready for use and, as a further precaution, asked Chairman James to recognize me if I asked for recognition during roll call.

When I conferred with the delegates I found a number of them in rebellion against Clark. They were afraid to risk voting for him any longer. I still pleaded with them, but when the roll was called, half or a little more voted for Wilson, but I still cast my ballot for Clark. Senator

---

* Mr. Bryan's change from Clark to Wilson was soon after endorsed by the Nebraska State Democratic Convention, showing that he was right in his interpretation of the spirit of the instructions from his constituents.

Hitchcock, who advocated instructions for Harmon in the Nebraska primary, came to me and said he would have to demand a poll of the delegation. I replied that in case a poll was taken I would take the platform and explain my vote. I was willing to continue voting for Clark if the delegation was not polled, but expecting at any time that I might be compelled to change my vote, I was not willing to announce a vote for him that I might have to take back at any time. I decided, therefore, to make the change at that time if the poll was taken. Senator Hitchcock insisted upon the poll and when my name was called I went to the platform and read the explanation of the change which I had prepared. It will be found in the Appendix.

As might have been expected, this change caused a commotion in the convention. The Clark delegates, with four ex-governors among them, sat just in front of the platform. None of them questioned me, but two other delegates, one from Mississippi and one from West Virginia, did. One asked whether I intended to support the candidate. I answered that that was a hypothetical question and that such a question was never favored in a court of law because it was difficult to put into the question all the conditions that might enter into the decision, but that I would answer his question by saying that I expected to support the nominee, whoever he was. Another asked how I could support the candidate if I was opposed to his nomination. I answered that the questioner, being a lawyer, ought to know that an attorney could defend his client after the crime was committed, but that he was not allowed to join the client in committing the crime.

Early in the afternoon Senator Stone arose in his place in the Missouri delegation. Suspecting that he intended to make some motion relating to the two thirds rule, I immediately went to the front of the platform (our delegation, while on the front row, was some distance to the left of the speaker) in order to be ready to make an objec-

tion. He asked unanimous consent to move to suspend the
rules and declare Mr. Clark the nominee of the convention,
basing his argument on the fact that he had received a
majority of the votes cast. Some one, I think from New
Jersey, objected and the roll call proceeded.

A little later in the afternoon some of the supporters of
Mr. Clark brought into the convention a banner on which
was reproduced a sentence that I had used in eulogizing
Mr. Clark when I spoke in his district in 1910. This caused
an uproar as it was carried through the aisles. It was
finally brought over to our delegation and caused such a
burst of feeling from some of our delegates that I feared
trouble might be precipitated. I immediately returned to
the platform with the intention of explaining the time and
the conditions under which the words were spoken and the
reasons why I did not feel that an opinion expressed then
required me to support Mr. Clark under the circumstances
that had developed. While Speaker James was trying to
secure order I stepped down from the platform to the
Missouri delegates to inquire of its leaders whether the men
carrying the banner were acting under their instructions.
They assured me that they were not responsible for it.
Finally Chairman James, acting wisely, I think, refused to
recognize me, at the same time, as I recall it, directing that
the banner be removed from the hall.

This was one of the exciting moments of the convention,
because it stirred up much feeling. I think in the excitement blows were exchanged in two or three instances. I
know that many of my friends feared for my personal safety.
The Texas delegation of forty was, I afterwards learned,
ready to lend assistance in case any attack was made upon
me. It was the only time in my life when I was in danger
of physical harm and, therefore, the only time when my
physical courage was tested, if test it could be called. The
thought of danger did not occur to me as I went among
those who were highly excited.

THE BALTIMORE CONVENTION

When Saturday night came the issue was still undecided. Wilson had gained enough to make Clark's nomination improbable and Clark still held enough to make the selection of Wilson uncertain.

From the time the convention met there were many delegates who favored my nomination, some under instructions for Clark and some under instructions for Wilson. I had aided in the election of many of these delegates, the anti-Harmon delegates from Ohio being under special obligation for the trip that I made through that state. One of the Ohio delegates voted for me until I asked him to refrain, pointing out that it was unfair to me to make it seem that I had only one friend in the convention when others were restrained from voting for me out of regard for my wishes. When the convention seemed to be settling down into a deadlock there were many who urged my nomination as a solution of the situation. But I felt that it was not proper for me to consider the question as long as there was any chance for any of the candidates who had been encouraged to enter by my announcement that I would not be a candidate, and I felt, too, that the action I had been compelled to take out of a sense of duty to the party had alienated some of those whose support was necessary to an election. I told all who inquired that nothing but a situation which made the whole convention regard my nomination as necessary justified my considering the nomination and that there had been no time when circumstances presented such a situation or promised it.

While hostilities were suspended during the Sabbath the messages continued to pour in from over the country and these at last crushed the opposition to Wilson and compelled his nomination.

When the convention entered upon the nomination of candidates for Vice-President a delegate from the District of Columbia presented my name for Vice-President. I had not been consulted about the matter and am not sure that

185

the nomination was made in good faith. I did not wait to inquire or to ascertain the sentiment of the delegates. I declined to be considered, embodying my reasons in a brief speech which will be found in the Appendix. When the names were being presented I made speeches seconding the nomination of two western men, Burke of North Dakota and Chamberlain of Oregon. I had no personal objection to Governor Marshall, but his support of Judge Parker for temporary chairman, his opposition to the initiative and referendum, and his attitude toward prohibition as shown in the campaign of 1908 seemed to me to raise issues that might endanger success of the party. While his views on the initiative and referendum and prohibition had not altered, these questions did not come before him during his term as Vice-President and I have admired the manner in which he presented the Democratic side of most of the big questions at issue. He made a very popular Vice-President.

CHAPTER XI

THE GRAPE JUICE INCIDENT

I HAVE mentioned my aversion to swearing as due to my mother's teachings, my father concurring; and of my aversion to gambling taught by my father, my mother concurring. I am indebted to both for a third moral lesson in which they joined so heartily that I am not able to emphasize the influence of either over the influence of the other. They both abstained from the use of intoxicating liquor and impressed upon me at a very early age the evils that follow from its use. Even before I had any clear understanding of the temperance question I began signing the pledge. I have no way of knowing at what age I first signed—my recollection does not run back so far— I only know that I have been signing since I can remember. I met, a few years ago, a temperance lecturer who told me that I was among the signers at his meeting when he spoke there in 1872; I was then twelve, but it had by that time become a habit with me. The formative influence of these early habits is well illustrated in this case.

My wife was brought up in the same way and the antipathy toward the use of liquor as a beverage at any time and in any form was so great that she joined me in excluding it from public dinners when I was Secretary of State as we had excluded it from our table in private life. It may be better to speak of the "Grape Juice Dinner" here than to refer to it later in recording my experiences in that office.

When President-elect Wilson invited me to Trenton I surmised the purpose of the invitation was to invite me to become a member of his Cabinet and I discussed with my wife the matter of serving liquors before meeting with the President. We were not willing to violate our custom in

187

this respect and to set such an example to others, and it was therefore understood that I should bring the matter to the attention of the President at the time in order that there might be no criticism later. After going over other matters connected with the office, I told him that there was one thing about which I felt concerned and that was whether he would regard the exclusion of intoxicating liquors from our table as an insurmountable objection to my assuming the duties of the office. He promptly responded that it was a matter upon which we could feel perfectly free to follow our own wishes. I said that we never had served it and as a matter of conscience did not wish to. The matter was never referred to again by the President in conversation with me.

Soon after I became Secretary of State we had occasion to entertain Ambassador Bryce at luncheon. In order to explain the absence of wine from the table I told him that Mrs. Bryan and I were departing from the official custom in this respect and that he was our first guest. He answered very cheerfully that he was a good person to begin on, as he did not use intoxicating liquors himself. He was preparing to leave Washington and not long after this we gave him a farewell luncheon to which all of the ambassadors were invited. Several Washington ladies were invited as luncheon companions for the ambassadors whose wives were not in the city. When Mrs. Bryan arranged the table she had a glass for grape juice, not that we thought of drawing a contrast between wine and grape juice, but because the glasses for plain and mineral water looked a little lonesome. At her suggestion, I explained to the guests very briefly the reason for our departure from the official custom, and stated that we hoped that our hospitality would be so cordial that the guests would not miss the wine. It was rather an embarrassing occasion to us, because we had no desire to emphasize our views on this subject and I felt quite relieved when the explanation was finished. To my

THE GRAPE JUICE INCIDENT

surprise, the guests applauded very heartily and we had a delightful time together. I did not mention the incident to the newspapers and it was some days before anything was said about it. When the facts were published, I was called upon for a statement, and the statement gradually found its way throughout the world.

The foreign comments were numerous and for the most part unfriendly. Some friend who had gathered a collection of these comments sent me his file. About the only friendly reference among them was from a Canadian paper which remarked that, from the criticisms made by the newspapers on the absence of wine from our table, one might suppose that the luncheon had been a bartenders' reunion.

A few months afterward when a Republican ambassador was closing up his accounts at the department before retiring from the office, he called upon me and with evident emotion thanked me for my action at the luncheon, especially referring to the harm done young men by the bad example set by the use of liquors by men in high official position.

Within two years the war had aroused so much interest in the liquor question in foreign nations that a number of the crowned heads of Europe were lining up against intoxicating drinks. Then I received my reward. The papers began to cartoon me as driving a water wagon with kings crowding each other for a seat on the vehicle.

CHAPTER XII

THE CHILDREN

WE have been fortunate in our children and grand-children. The former are three in number, Ruth Baird, now Mrs. Reginald Owen, born October 2, 1885; William Jennings Bryan, Jr., born June 24, 1889; and Grace Dexter, now Mrs. Richard L. Hargreaves, born February 17, 1891.

Ruth came within a day of celebrating our first wedding anniversary. She was a precocious child and her parents and grandparents were kept busy expressing surprise at evidences of her early intelligence.

What a marvel a child is! It comes into the world with such perfection displayed in its mechanism, is so helpless, and yet so full of possibilities for good or for evil. It gives to one woman a sweet consciousness of motherhood and to one man a sense of responsibility otherwise never known before. Before its tiny hands can lift a featherweight, it has drawn two hearts closer together; its innocent prattle echoes through two lives and its influence upon its parents is almost as moulding as their influence upon it.

I think my wife never before looked so sweet as she did when she brought Ruth downstairs for the first time. The wrapper which she wore that day was long and flowing and she made me think of a Madonna. In fact, seeing a copy of Bodenhausen's painting of the Madonna a few weeks afterwards in an art gallery in Kansas City—the Madonna arrayed in a gown of almost the same tint as the gown my wife had worn—so impressed me by the resemblance that I took the picture home with me. It hung upon our walls until our son was married and desired to have it for his own home.

One of the distinct recollections of Ruth's babyhood was

the time when she was old enough to distinguish the different members of the family. Mrs. Bryan's father and I would often be sitting near the mother when the baby was being washed and dressed. When her night garments were removed she would hand them sometimes to the father and sometimes to the grandfather. It was an anxious moment when we were in suspense while she decided to which she would hand the garment. She was quite impartial, bestowing the favor on first one, then the other as if she thought favoritism to one might hurt the feelings of the other.

Ruth, when about three years old, delivered a prayer which we have always remembered as illustrating at that early age a keen sense of discrimination, as well as indicating a positive opinion. It was in the fall of 1888 and I was away from home campaigning. When it came time to go to bed she was irritated about some happening of the day and refused to say her usual prayer, which began, "Now I lay me down to sleep," and ended with, "God bless Papa, Mamma, Grandma, Grandpa, and all of Grandma Bryan's folks, Amen." Her mother tried persuasion along several lines, but in vain. Finally, thinking to appeal to her affections, she said, "Poor Papa is away on the train and might get hurt and his little girl will not say any prayer for him." This touched Ruth's heart. She went over to the bed, knelt down and said, "Dear Lord, take care of Papa—not Mamma nor Grandma nor anybody else, just Papa. Amen." It reminded me of Lincoln's letter to Horace Greeley in which he so specifically expressed his intentions and carefully negatived everything else.

Ruth early gave evidence of literary ability. She wrote stories which showed imagination. One day when eight or nine years old she came to her mother and asked whether it would be better to have the hero save the heroine from a fire or from drowning. Mrs. Bryan expressed a preference for a rescue from fire. In a little while Ruth had her story

191

completed with a thrilling description of the rescue of a girl from a burning building.

It was about this time that she revealed her ambition and, at the same time, her doubts as to whether she would realize it. She was confined to her bed by an attack of measles. One morning when I took her breakfast to her room and sat by her while she ate it, I said, "Ruth, what would you like to do when you are grown?" She answered spiritedly, "I would like to write stories and books"—and then she added in a melancholy tone, "But I expect I'll get married and raise a family, like Mamma and Mrs. Schwind."

It was during this period, also, that she returned from the Sunday school one day very much disgusted and threatened not to go any more, giving as her excuse, "They don't teach righteousness; they just teach geography."

I may add here that Ruth always showed a discretion rather unusual for her years. In the campaign of 1896 when she was eleven she was, of course, often questioned by strangers. One day a man stopped her in the street and asked her whether she thought her father would be elected. She replied, "I think he will get a good many votes on D Street" (the street on which we lived), "but I do not know about the rest of the country."

After nine years in the Nebraska public school, two years at Monticello Seminary (Illinois), and two years in the State University of Nebraska, came Ruth's marriage the day following her eighteenth birthday anniversary, October 3, 1903. She had a son and a daughter by this first marriage.

In the autumn of 1907 she made her first venture on the lecture platform, filling engagements for the Extension Department of the State University of Nebraska and under other auspices.

Her second marriage occurred on the third of May, 1910. Reginald Altham Owen was a lieutenant in the Royal Engineers of the British Army at the time of their marriage.

THE CHILDREN

He served with distinction in the World War, throughout the entire Dardanelles Campaign and the three years of the Egypt and Palestine campaign. His health was so seriously impaired by his war service that he was retired from the service in 1924 after prolonged sick leave.

Major and Mrs. Owen's home since the conclusion of the war has been in Miami, Florida.

Ruth has during the past five years extended her lecture tours and achieved considerable success to which she has added some prominence in literary work. Her daughter Ruth, who was born September 28, 1904, grew from a bright child to a very attractive young woman. She was married June 20, 1923, to William Painter Meeker, of Baltimore, Maryland, and Miami, Florida, only son of our nearest neighbors in Miami. Their daughter Ruth, born June 30, 1924, is our only and much beloved great-grandchild.

Mrs. Owen's son, John Baird Bryan, was born November 16, 1905. He was a most interesting child and has developed talent for art and poetry, which he is disposed to cultivate. The two younger children of Major and Mrs. Owen are not yet old enough to give indication of their natural bent. Reginald Bryan, who was born in London April 14, 1913, gives evidence of a strong will, a quality of great value when well directed. Helen Rudd, born August 3, 1920, is a very precocious child with unusual poise and self-reliance.

William, our only son, was born on June 24, 1889. He was what is called "a regular fellow." He was one hundred per cent boy—never bad, but always mischievous. He could get into dirt more quickly after he was sent out washed and cleanly dressed, and into more different kinds of dirt than any boy I have ever known. This may be because I was never as well acquainted with another boy.

When Ruth was a baby she was a little thin—at least, not fat. William was quite a fat baby. Mrs. Bryan says that when Ruth was a child and rather thin I expressed a preference for thin children; but that when William came I thought he was just fat enough to look well.

Mrs. Bryan took care of the children herself. As the care of the children increased she turned over more of the domestic work to others in order that she might have entire charge of the children. She put them to bed and read to them until they went to sleep. Often after she had cleansed William of the dirt stains of the day and read him to sleep, she would lead me to the room that I might admire our young hopeful, exclaiming as she looked upon him with loving eyes, "Isn't he sweet when he is asleep?"

How a boy ever lives through the accidents of childhood is a mystery. William fell down the stairway and was insensible for several hours, but he was soon over it and ready to take another risk. One day his mother was badly frightened when she looked out and saw him working his way along the telephone wires some distance from the house. When we took him out with us on visits to friends, the conversation was often interrupted by a cry of alarm, some member of the family finding William up on the roof or in some other place of danger.

He had reached the age of eleven by the time of the second campaign in 1900. By that time he had become an excellent swimmer. I might add that Mrs. Bryan had taken upon herself the task of teaching all the children how to swim. Like all swimmers, he was fond of diving. During a few days' stay in Chicago the newspaper men, who take such an interest in every member of the family of the candidate, discovered his fondness for the water and gave a good deal of attention to his accomplishments, not diminishing in the least the sensational features. At one time he was described as hanging out of an upper window of a tall building and being rescued by General Wheeler.

A few years ago I discovered a photograph of William at this busy age. I had it framed and put on his mother's

194

desk as a reminder of the anxiety she cheerfully endured during the superactive years of William's youth.

William was nearly seven at the time of the death of Mrs. Bryan's mother. His affection manifested itself in a bit of consolation that we have often looked back to with amusement. He went up to his mother when she was weeping and, putting his arms around her neck, said, "Mamma, when you feel sad, just think of me."

At another time when he was just recovering from a punishment for some misdemeanor, he sobbed out a warning to his mother, "If I died in the night, you would not feel so gay."

Like Ruth, he was studious enough to pass his examinations, but was not at the head of the class. I had hoped that he would early manifest an interest in public speaking as I had, but instead of showing an unusual interest in it, he manifested an aversion to speaking. Mrs. Bryan went over one day to the school to hear him speak a piece. When the teacher called on him to do his part, he sank down into his chair and clutched its arms. After his mother had waited for a few moments for her son to immortalize himself as a speaker, the teacher gave up in despair and said, "William will speak *next* Friday."

I was somewhat surprised, therefore, when my wife read me a letter from the superintendent of Culver Military School which he was attending, stating that William was studying public speaking. A few months afterwards, I met the great evangelist, Rev. J. Wilbur Chapman, and he told me that his son and mine were in the same elocution class; adding that he had promised his boy fifty dollars if he would surpass William in speaking. His boy replied that that was impossible, that not one of the boys could do better. This was the beginning of his efforts to express himself "on his feet." I found afterwards as I read his speeches and heard them that he had an analytical mind, logical arrangement of his arguments, persuasive delivery, and a sense of humor that enabled him to enliven his addresses.

Owing to the fact that his betrothed, Miss Helen Berger, with whom he fell in love when he was quite young and to whom he had been engaged for some years, found it necessary on account of her health to reside in Arizona, he was married before he finished school and continued his studies at the University of Arizona at Tucson, where he graduated. He afterwards became regent of the University by appointment by Governor Hunt and reappointed by Governor Campbell.

I was very much pleased to learn that he was made director of the Y.M.C.A. and a member of the Democratic Committee of Tucson the same week. I accepted it as an indication that he was interested in the two lines of work, religion and politics, which not only do not conflict but are entirely consistent.

After graduating he studied law at Georgetown Law School. He was elected president of his class, but in a few months he was compelled to return to Arizona on account of his wife's health and he resumed his law study there. After his admission to the bar he became assistant to the United States Attorney under United States Attorney John Flynn.

William was married in June 24, 1909, to Helen Virginia Berger, of Milwaukee, Wisconsin. They have three children —all daughters: Mary Scholes, born April 7, 1910, Helen Virginia, born August 13, 1911, and Elizabeth Baird, born December 31, 1914. They are as charming a trio as one could find, but three distinct types.

In 1920 William and his family removed to Los Angeles, California, which is their present residence.

[PUBLISHERS' NOTE. In publishing these unfinished Memoirs of Mr. Bryan, we are sure that no omission would fill him with more regret than his failure to complete the chapter which tells of his children.

He was called from this task before he had written of his younger and much loved daughter Grace Dexter (Mrs. Richard L. Hargreaves of Berkeley Hills, California).

Herself born in the midst of a political campaign, Mrs. Hargreaves has always been deeply interested in politics. As a child she took part in all the children's parades with great zest and in later years followed her father's political work with keen interest and sympathy.

During Mr. Bryan's second term in Congress she was critically ill with pneumonia, which left her in a very weakened condition. She became a great anxiety to her parents, and several years of special care and sojourn in warm climates was required to restore her to strength.

She was educated at home by a governess and afterwards in the Lincoln, Nebraska, schools, and at Hollins Institute (Virginia).

She was married in June 7, 1911, to Richard Lewis Hargreaves, of Lincoln, Nebraska, and to them three children have been born: Margaret, born March 3, 1914; Bryan, born September 7, 1915; and Evelyn Mary, born October 16, 1920, the latter being the tenth and youngest of Mr. Bryan's grandchildren.]

CHAPTER XIII

Friendships

SO much is flippantly told about the fair-weather friends in politics who flock about the successful candidate and then desert him in times of trial, that I shall take this opportunity to record a few instances of heroes who came under my personal observation. I omit the names out of consideration for those who had been personally connected with the incidents and who may not regard them in the same spirit in which I regard them.

First I mention a Congressman and one of the Ways and Means Committee. He had retired from Congress in 1896 and resumed charge of a large mercantile business in the town in which he resided. He was an advocate of bimetallism when in Congress and took a large interest in my first Presidential campaign. He was one of the well-to-do men of his city and a director in the bank in which he kept his store account. Like most merchants, he enjoyed a credit in the bank and borrowed money from time to time to discount his bills.

In the midst of the campaign he was called before the directors of his own bank and informed that his interest in me was injuring the bank and then he was told that his notes could not be carried any longer if he continued to support my candidacy. He was put to a test to which I have never been subjected. There has never been a time since I was grown when my bread and butter depended upon the will or favor of any other person, and therefore never a time when I incurred any financial risk in exercising political independence. It was not so with the friend of whom I am speaking. He knew that he could not at that time secure loans elsewhere if the bank of which he was a director refused to accommodate him, but he did not hesitate for a moment.

FRIENDSHIPS

He replied, "Gentlemen, you can bankrupt me, but you cannot take from me my right to vote as I please."

Of course, the directors dared not carry out their threat, but their bluff gave one friend a chance to show the mettle that was in him. Until he was called to his reward, I counted him as one of the inner circle of my friends.

Another illustration is taken from among my New York friends. I appreciate them the more because the coercion was there at its maximum and the support to be found in companionship at its minimum. As far back as 1893, the campaign of 1896 cast its shadow before it. I spoke at Cooper Union in the fall of that year, my subject being the unconditional repeal of the Sherman Law then before Congress. The hall was crowded and I learned a few days afterward the following incident relating to a man then and since prominent in the business world.

Not being able to find a seat, he was standing in the aisle near the door when an acquaintance on the platform spied him and invited him to a seat. A place on the platform did not necessarily indicate sympathy with the speaker, but one of the papers next morning gave a list of those on the platform and included the gentleman of whom I am speaking. I was about to say friend, but at the time of the incident I was not personally acquainted with him.

Upon reading the list this gentleman's banker sent for him and called his attention to the fact that he had been mentioned among those who sat on the platform. He explained the situation, assuring the banker that he was not there by pre-arrangement or for the purpose of being counted among those specially interested, but the explanation did not satisfy the banker and he notified this gentleman that they could not carry loans for those who gave the weight of their names to so disreputable a cause and insisted that he immediately pay a note of $25,000 which the bank held against him. Fortunately, he was able to do so without embarrassment and immediately complied with the request.

It is needless to say that the demand made a deep impression upon him and that that impression was not favorable to the bankers' side of the question. During the campaign of 1896 he took a prominent part, and Mrs. Bryan and I had the pleasure of being guests later in his beautiful home on the Hudson. From that time to this his sympathies have been with the masses on all the economic questions that have arisen.

A Massachusetts friend reported to me an experience through which he passed in the campaign of 1896. He was engaged in manufacturing upon a considerable scale and carried a credit of some $20,000 or more at his local bank. In the campaign of 1896 he was a Democrat and outspoken though not active in the support of the ticket. His banker sent for him and asked him whether he was supporting my candidacy. He answered that he expected to vote for me, but was not active beyond that. The banker informed him that they could not lend financial aid to those who were opposing the bank's policy and asked him to take up his notes. This he did and then went out and spoke for me during the rest of the campaign. He, too, has ever since that time continued his political activity.

A New York lawyer who had been a delegate to the Chicago Convention returned to the metropolis and entered the campaign. He was one of the delegates who had refused to join the New York financiers in support of the gold ticket. He was attorney for a bank, and the bank on reading of his attitude sent for him, withdrew all its cases from him and asked him to change his deposit to another bank. He complied with the request, opened his account in a bank not so illiberal in its politics and took an active part in the campaign until it closed.

This is the only case I know of where a bank compelled a depositor to withdraw his account. After the election was over the bank sent for the attorney, asked that the unpleasantness be forgotten and reëmployed him. In New Jersey he afterward became a member of Congress and became quite conspicuous in public life.

I have a very delightful recollection of a conductor on one of the railroads running into Lincoln. "Pat" was the name by which he was known and it was spoken with affection by the multitude who knew him as a man of character—the kind of man who attaches his friends to him by hooks of steel. I became acquainted with Pat in my early trips through the first district even before I became a candidate for Congress. I had no more ardent supporter than he in my races for Congress and for the Senate.

In 1896, when so much pressure was brought by corporations upon their employees, Pat was called into the office and informed that the railroad was strongly in favor of Mr. McKinley's election and that they would expect him to give the benefit of his influence.

Did they intimidate him? Not for a moment. He replied: "Your salary pays for my services as conductor, but it does not include my citizenship. That is my own. I vote as I please." Pat continued to be a Democrat and he also continued to be a conductor.

In my own city one of the banks required a business man to agree to support the Republican candidate in order to continue a loan at the bank. He told of the instance himself. Upon my return from a trip around the world a dinner was given me. This merchant, whom we had known from the time I moved to Lincoln, asked whether he could secure a ticket, adding: "I have voted for Mr. Bryan at every election except one. I voted for him for Congress twice and for the Senate and would have voted for him in 1896 but for the fact that I owed a large amount to the —— bank. Just before the election Mr. ——, the president of the bank, refused to extend the loan unless I would agree to vote for McKinley. It would have meant bankruptcy if I had refused and so I promised to vote for McKinley and, having promised, I did so, but by 1900 I had so far reduced

201

my indebtedness that I was independent and I voted for Mr. Bryan that year."

Shortly after the election I met on the train Mr. Yost, an Omaha business man who was president of the Lincoln Telephone Company. Introducing the subject himself, he said, "I have a friend of yours working for me at Lincoln."

Guessing whom he had in mind, I said, "Do you mean Mr. ——?"

"Yes," he replied. "I went down to Lincoln just before the election and told him that we were very much interested in Mr. McKinley's election and hoped he would do what he could to help him. He said, 'Mr. Yost, your company has been very good to me and I do not want to do anything that would injure it. If you think that my support of Mr. Bryan will hurt your company, I will resign.' After hearing his answer, what do you think I told him?"

"What?" I asked.

"I told him that if he did not vote for you we would discharge him."

I have often recalled this incident because it illustrates an important truth, namely, that a frank and firm defense of one's political rights is much better at all times than an evasion of the subject or the practice of deception.

In recording my political experiences I dwell with greatest pleasure upon the friendships formed in early years. I was in no position to reward men for what they did for me, so that their acts of kindness were wholly unselfish and were prompted by a devotion which I have come to regard as the most beautiful thing in American politics. We are too prone to explain service as selfish and kind acts as prompted by a hope of reward. The prevailing opinion of political support has been put into poetry in the description of those who "crook the pregnant hinges of the knee, where thrift may follow fawning." This may be an accurate description of some self-seeking politicians, but it is a slander upon the virtuous masses to suggest that what they do is done from other than the noblest spirit.

When George Hopkins, of Nemaha County, Nebraska, wins a place in my memory by taking me in a sulky some thirteen miles from Peru to Auburn after a night meeting and then appears regularly at every meeting held in this county for a quarter of a century and gives weeks of time to campaigning for me no matter to what office I aspire, it can only be accounted for by similarity of political ideals which made him feel that my campaigns were really his campaigns also.

When Will Glenn, of Knox County, takes me in a buggy fifty miles in a single day and night and puts me on a departing train a little before daybreak, it is proof of his heart interest in the issue at stake.

When a farmer in the center of the state gets out of bed in the middle of the night when we have lost our way, rides ten miles before us, and then when we come in sight of the lights of our destination, turns back, refusing compensation with the remark, spoken in a tone that indicated that even the offer hurt his feelings: "Do you think I would do this for money? I am a Bryan man," one catches something of the sentiment upon which campaigns are built and can better understand how it is possible for millions of people to coöperate without organization but actuated by a common impulse.

These incidents could be continued indefinitely; there has never been a time when in Nebraska or somewhere else in the United States I have not had occasion to be proud of the average man and his influence in politics. The names of the humble heroes in political battles of the United States is legion. Their names are unrecorded, but those whom they so faithfully support receive the glory. I cannot forget these soldiers upon whom the brunt of the battle falls.

As I look back over the years I see the face of one of the most loyal friends that any political leader ever had. His name was John Ahern, a big, brawny Irishman. He was nearly, if not quite, six feet four inches in height and broad in proportion. His face was round and no beard concealed the friendliness that beamed from every feature. I met him in 1888 when I made my first trip to Richardson County, Nebraska. He lived some twenty miles from Fall City, the county seat. Partly because his size made him a conspicious figure in the crowd and partly because of the devotion which he manifested, I came to look for him in the crowd whenever I spoke in his county. And I do not recall a meeting that he did not attend.

One night I went home with him and stayed all night. It is a rare treat to drop in upon one of these country friends, a treat in which I indulge myself whenever opportunity offers, but the opportunities have been all too few. Time and again at Chautauquas as I have looked into the faces of the old men for whom the front seats are generally reserved, I have picked out one of these American sovereigns, a well-informed voter whom an army could not terrorize and whom the federal treasury could not buy, and regretted that on account of the briefness of my stay I could not step up to him and say, "May I go and spend the night with you?" These are the common people, the people to whom the Bible pays the highest compliment it ever pays to any class when it says that the common people heard Christ gladly. It is by communion with such as these that one is assured of the impregnable strength of the nation and it is from such as these that one can learn the drift of the public sentiment and best predict with certainty the things to be.

But to return to Ahern. In the fall of 1894, when I was a candidate for the United States Senate, I made my usual trip to Richardson County and spoke to a great meeting in Fall City. When the crowd had dispersed Uncle John, as he was familiarly called, came up to encourage me by a grasp of his large warm hand and went with me to the hotel not far distant. We sat down and talked a little while about the political prospects and then prepared to start out to his country home. He hesitated for a moment and then, taking me by the arm, led me out of the hotel office and into the broad hallway to the farthest corner. Speaking in an undertone, he said:

"If we carry the legislature"—this was in 1888 before the popular election of senators—"I will come to Lincoln during the session. I do not know that I can do any good, but there may be some member whom I can influence.

"And then," lowering his voice, "if we can get you into the Senate you can take care of yourself."

I do not recall a more fatherly expression that that of this dear friend. He had done all he could for me in two Congressional campaigns and now he had a chance to aid in an election, which, if successful, would give me a six-year term in the Senate, and he felt that two terms in Congress and a term in the Senate ought to put me on such secure ground that I would be assured a permanent place in public life.

Sixteen years later, in 1910—sixteen years during which his unwavering devotion had expressed itself in three Presidential campaigns—the question of prohibition became an issue in Nebraska. I came out in support of county option, as is recorded in another chapter. Mr. Ahern was not only not a prohibitionist but he lacked something of being a teetotaler. I never saw him under the influence of liquor, but he drank with some regularity and possibly, when political excitement ran high, with some freedom. The newspapers soon reported my activity on the side of county option and one of the Democrats of Richardson County brought the matter to the attention of Ahern. The conversation was reported to me as follows:

"Uncle John, have you heard that Billy has come out for county option?"

"No," Uncle John answered in surprise.

"Well, he has," said his informant.

WILLIAM JENNINGS BRYAN

"Is that so?" replied Uncle John.

"What do you think of Billy now?" continued his informant.

"I am for him, wet or dry," responded my Irish friend. And he was.

Little differences like that did not disturb his friendship; it was built upon a more solid foundation.

A few years after this Mr. Ahern passed away, as I learned during a visit in Nebraska. By this time the demands of national politics kept me away from my home state most of the time. The only offset to the pleasure that comes from a large circle of friends is the frequency with which one is called upon to mourn when "from love's shining circle the gems drop away."

In 1916 the question of state prohibition became the dominant issue in Nebraska and I made a tour of the state in support of that movement. In the course of my travels I spoke at Shubert, the nearest Richardson County town to Mr. Ahern's farm. I spoke from an auto and told the group of listeners that I was more interested in prohibition than I ever was in my own candidacy and needed their support more than I had needed it in previous campaigns. When my speech was finished four men filed up to the auto, all over six feet in height, and informed me that they were sons of John Ahern. I greeted them as cordially as I had their father, and after telling them how much I missed his presence, asked them if they were with me in my fight for prohibition. They all answered very positively in the affirmative. I was greatly pleased to find that the sons had inherited from their father the friendship that had so long existed between the elder Ahern and myself.

My last campaign in Nebraska was made in the spring of 1920 when I was a candidate for delegate for Nebraska to the convention at San Francisco. In my tour from my old first district I passed Ahern's home and detoured a mile or so to visit the family. In a very few minutes the boys had come in from the field, and the children, including the oldest daughter, who was a cripple, assured me that they would be on hand to help make me a delegate.

Possibly the reader, if he has never been in politics, may feel that I have devoted too much space to one of my million and a half political friends, but I single him out as illustrative of a very large number from whom I have received so many manifestations of confidence and affection. It is to such as these that I owe the political opportunities which have come to me, opportunities without which it would have been impossible for me to be identified in a large way with great national problems—opportunities by the improvement of which I have been able to accomplish whatever may be placed to my account in the final reckoning.

Another friend lived in Dawson, in the same county, Richardson. He gave touching evidence of his devotion. Jerry Fenton was my friend and supporter from the time I entered politics in Nebraska until he died. During my Congressional campaigns my picture was used, as is customary, in the advertisement of meetings, and either in this way or by direct request Mr. Fenton secured my likeness and had it hung on the wall of his bedroom. My trip around the world was commenced in the fall of 1905, fifteen years after my first race for Congress. Mr. Fenton had supported me, therefore, in two Congressional campaigns, one senatorial and two Presidential campaigns. He, too, was always present at my meetings and was an influential factor in our party. When I returned in 1906 his family physician told me of an incident that I have remembered as one of the sweetest expressions of that affection which is not infrequent in political life. During my absence abroad I kept in touch with intimate friends through my paper, the *Commoner*, which published altogether more than forty letters written in various countries that I visited. While I was away Mr. Fenton fell ill, so ill that at times his life was despaired of. On one occasion he had a sinking spell which it was feared would speedily end in his death. After his priest had called and administered the sacraments of the Church, the patient, sustained by his faith, calmly awaited the end. During this period of suspense, while the members of the family stood by in helpless anxiety, Mr. Fenton called the doctor to the bedside and whispered to him, pointing to the wall, "When Mr. Bryan gets back tell him that his picture was before me to the last." One incident of such devotion outweighs a multitude of cruel and unjust criticisms.